BLUE RIDGE CHINA TODAY

A Comprehensive Ident   Today's Collector

Frances and John Ruffin

Blue Ridge
Underglaze Hand Painted

Schiffer Publishing Ltd

77 Lower Valley Road, Atglen, PA 19310

In Loving Memory of Theresa and Frank Robilio

Dedicated to the Employees of Southern Potteries 1920-1957

On the cover: FRENCH PEASANT Maple Leaf Relish

Copyright © 1997 by Frances and John Ruffin

Printed in Hong Kong

ISBN: 0-7643-0206-X

Designed by "Sue"

Published by Schiffer Publishing, Ltd.
77 Lower Valley Road
Atglen, PA 19310
Phone: (610) 593-1777
Fax: (610) 593-2002
Please write for a free catalog.
This book may be purchased from the publisher.
Please include $2.95 for shipping.
Try your bookstore first.

We are interested in hearing from authors with book ideas on related subjects.

Library of Congress Cataloging-in-Publication Data

Ruffin, Frances.
    Blue Ridge china today: a comprehensive identification and price guide for today's collector/Frances and John Ruffin.
        p. cm.
    Includes bibliographical references and index.
    ISBN 0-7643-0206-X
    1. Southern Potteries Inc.--Catalogs. 2. Blue Ridge dinner ware--Catalogs. 3. Pottery, American--Tennessee--Erwin--Catalogs. I. Ruffin, John. II. Title.
NK4210.S623A4 1997
738.3'09768'982--dc20
                                    96-41048
                                    CIP

Acknowledgments

A very sincere and heartfelt thanks to fellow Blue Ridge collectors who allowed us to photograph their unbelievable collections. You welcomed us into your homes, answered our numerous questions, encouraged us, and very often fed us delicious meals on Blue Ridge dinnerware, of course. You will be forever in our hearts and prayers.

We would also like to thank those who helped us from afar, especially our friends in Erwin. You sent us photographs, information, suggestions, E-mail, and encouragement. You also will never be forgotten. We are also grateful to friends and fellow collectors, who searched antique shops, malls, and estate sales to find one more special piece.

Of course, an enormous thanks to our loved ones. To Johnny and Lisa for epitomizing the true spirit of all Blue Ridge collectors: Shop 'til you drop. To Cheryl for patiently and endlessly recording and editing this manuscript. To Andrea for advising us financially and professionally. To Dana and Roby for giving us Elizabeth, our motivation for collecting children's dinnerware. To Teri and Tom for their undying love of dogs, flowers, and the wonders of nature.

To each of you listed on the following page and to our anonymous contributors, we say:

Thank You!

Sincerely,
Frances & John Ruffin

Contributors

Antique Mall of Texas
Joyce & Paul Arbaugh
Austin Antique Mall
Faye Bailey
Lester Bailey
Virginia & Lincoln Barber
Linda Beamer
Sue & Jeff Beaulieu
Eunice & Carl Booker
Larry Boxum
Nelda & Benny Brewer
Marie & Mike Compton
Mildred & Jack Conley
Jerry Courson
The Hanging Elephant Antique Mall
Charles Edwards
Erwin Chamber of Commerce
Erwin Public Library
Erwin Record
Martha Erwin
Mary & Ray Farley
Ann Gardner
Emily & Jerry Gordon
Jane Greig
Cindy Harris
Wanda & John Hashe
Mary Elena Kirk
Heritage Museum
Madelyn Kimmel-Holley

Eileen Jones
Teri & Tom Jones
Winnie Keillor
Rene' & Danny Keplinger
Samuel Koehler
Lands End
Judy E. Lewis
Edythe Manfield
Gwen & Otis Martin
Eloise & David McGinnis
Jay Parker
Negatha & Earl Peterson
Dana & Roby Redwine
Andrea Ruffin
Cheryl Ruffin
Lisa & John Ruffin
E.C. Sellors
Eddie Shelton
Wanda Shelton
Len Skiles
Linda Smith
Kim & Bryan Snyder
Southern Potteries Employees
Gail E. Taylor
Jo & Cliff Thompson
Walmart Photo Processors, Round Rock, TX
Sue Walsh
Bruce Wheeler
Wanda & Bob Woods

CONTENTS

Introduction

Once again, Blue Ridge China occupies a prominent place in the hearts and homes of Americans. This unique, hand painted pottery, produced long ago in the Blue Ridge mountains of Tennessee, has even found its way to South America and Germany. Our book, *Blue Ridge Today*, is a trip back to Erwin, Tennessee as well as a comprehensive guide designed to help you identify a pattern and estimate its value.

Patterns in **Chapter 3: Floral & Foliage**, with few exceptions, have been arranged by shape. Patterns in other chapters have been grouped according to theme. In most cases, we have placed serving and accessory pieces with their respective patterns. Many accessory pieces complement Colonial and Candlewick patterns, therefore we placed them following the Colonial floral patterns and before the Candlewick floral patterns. We combined Skyline and Trailway since many patterns are common to both shapes. Matching glassware and coordinating linen, made by various companies, are interspersed throughout the book. Likewise photographs of backstamps were placed with the pieces so stamped. Additional backstamp information is available in the Appendix. Interestingly, a study of the backstamps used by the pottery indicates a chronological pattern, although some backstamps appear to have been used during unexpected periods of production. Additionally, reissue of popular patterns, such as CHRISTMAS TREE, results in different backstamps on almost identical patterns. The backstamps coincided with subtle differences in painting, such as the color of a bow.

Our research involved firsthand inquiry in Erwin, where it all began and still continues. We spoke directly with people who had been employed by the pottery, especially those individuals who were knowledgeable concerning day-to-day operations, design and painting of patterns, and office and marketing procedures. We then proceeded to review all available written sources which contained information on the history of the pottery, beginning with the Clinchfield China era and ending with the close of the pottery. Although actual pottery records, reportedly destroyed, were not available, sufficient data was available for our purpose.

Next, we thoroughly reviewed all known sources containing Blue Ridge patterns, including a number of magazine and catalog advertisements. Using our extensive collection as a point of reference, we evaluated the reliability of both color and black and white photographs. We found color photographs to be helpful, while black and white photographs were only minimally so. Because most original pattern names were not available, patterns have been assigned names over the years. We attempted therefore, not only to identify patterns by previously assigned names, but to catalog those patterns that have acquired more than one name. We also felt it was important to reveal the pottery and retail pattern names and numbers whenever known because of the interesting link to the past. A list of known pattern numbers, found on many but not all vegetable bowls, is included in the Index.

Finally, we assigned names to patterns only when extensive research did not confirm an existing name. Whenever applicable, we added "variant" or "color" to a known pattern when it appeared that a modification, not a new pattern, had occurred. Note that names we assigned have been enclosed in quotation marks. As requested by collectors, we used actual flower or fruit names whenever possible. We also encouraged contributors of unidentified patterns to suggest appropriate names. Additionally, we have taken the liberty of naming some patterns after former employees of Southern Potteries.

Identification of patterns is not always an easy process. We have been most successful using a method based upon shape, type of pattern, and color. Since our book has been designed to facilitate your identification of patterns, it is suggested that you try the following procedure: First, identify the shape *(see Chapter 3)*. Next, proceed to the section showing the type of pattern you are seeking. For example, if you have a yellow sunflower on the piecrust shape, turn to the piecrust section in the floral pattern chapter and proceed to the pages with yellow multi-petal flowers. If your pattern closely resembles, but is not identical to one you see there, check to see if the pieces are comparable. For example, where we have shown a bread and butter plate, which does not contain a full pattern, we have described the rest of the pattern. If your pattern is definitely not shown there, go through the shapes in other sections and look for yellow flowers. Remember that variations were necessary when going from one shape to another in order to fit the flat, fluted, or perhaps crimped style. Look for distinguishing features found in many Blue Ridge patterns. For example, the deep tuck in the center of BOURBON ROSE is a characteristic found with this pattern. However, when adapted to the piecrust shape, it was apparently necessary that some changes in placement be made by the painters. Although color is a must in identifying, photographs often do not reflect the exact colors, hues, and slight pattern variations one finds on actual pieces of china.

To further aid you in identifying a pattern, especially on accessory pieces, we have given sizes whenever relevant. Keep in mind, that sizes vary due to a number of factors including the necessity to periodically replace molds that were used in the large amount of production that Southern experienced.

Finally, you asked, and we tried, to separate apples from cherries. We examined the patterns carefully, often discounting actual size of fruit portrayed. We looked instead to the shape, composition (i.e., variegated) and color of the leaves and stems. For example, strawberry leaves are quite fluffy, so they are easily recognized. Likewise, if you examine them closely, cherry stems are usually thin, firm and slightly curved. Many Blue Ridge patterns show apples as nearly flat on the bottom, while cherries often were painted with slightly pointed bottoms. Regardless of our consensus, we retained previous pattern names and classifications, but recorded our findings for your consideration. Let us know if you agree with our classifications of these as well as other puzzling fruit replications such as figs and pomegranates.

While prices for rare and unusual pieces continue to escalate, many Blue Ridge pieces remain quite affordable for today's collector. Fortunately, dinnerware sets in many patterns can be assembled for daily use in a price range comparable to today's offerings. Many decorative pieces are also still available at reasonable prices.

All suggested prices are for mint pieces, even when photographs indicate otherwise. The average prices listed with the photographs represent only that - average prices. Price estimations are based on an extensive inquiry into current prices throughout the United States. We considered mail order and E-mail price lists, compiled and evaluated price surveys sent to dealers throughout the United States, and consulted with collectors and dealers throughout the country. Additionally, we used our extensive shopping experiences to temper (adjust) prices whenever they appeared unrealistic. Our cumulative findings are presented in the Index for your consideration. In no way do they represent the absolute value of any or all items. We invite your comments and comparison prices.

Chapter 1
History of
Blue Ridge China

In 1916, the Carolina, Clinchfield, and Ohio Railroad selected Erwin, a small town in northeastern Tennessee, as the site for a pottery. The railroad was attempting to develop commercial enterprises along its lines as sources of revenue. Jack Conley, a retired railroader still residing in Erwin, recalls that raw materials-coal to fire the kilns, larkspur for making pottery glaze, and kaolin clay to form the pottery-were transported by a trunk rail line to the pottery. Finished products were then hauled by train to major rail distribution centers for transport across the country.

The railroad, which had established machine shops in Erwin, decided that the town was situated in a uniquely beautiful natural setting and deserved more than random residential and commercial development. In 1916, Grosvenor Atterbury, a New York City architect, was engaged by the railroad's land holding affiliate, Holston Corporation, to draw up a planned community. Two basic house plans were utilized to construct approximately fifty homes intended to house pottery employees. Rather than sell the lots in their planned community, the company built homes as rental units in order to control land usage and influence others to follow their lead in developments throughout the town. These homes still stand today, although most have undergone renovations over the years and are now privately owned.

The pottery was constructed in 1916 along the traditional lines of potteries of the day-one long building housing seven beehive kilns. Two additional kilns were added later. In the earliest days of the new pottery, local artisans were trained in gold lining, a popular method for decoration of china at that time. The new potteries' first commercial production of china occurred in 1917. At that time, the work force consisted of around one hundred employees.

Early operators for the new pottery were brought from Ohio and West Virginia by E.J. Owens, who owned a pottery in Sebring, Ohio, to initiate the production lines at the new plant. It is believed that the Owens family actually owned the pottery in Erwin from the outset.

Southern Potteries went public in 1920 when it received its corporate charter and stock totaling $500,000 was initially offered for sale. Charles W. Foreman, an associate of Owens in Ohio, bought the pottery outright in 1922. Foreman is credited with the introduction and perfection of the hand painting techniques which were to characterize Blue Ridge China in future years.

From 1917 through 1938, patterns were primarily applied to the bisque (the fired clay-like blank shapes) by use of decals, many of which were commonly used by other china producers of the period. Beginning in 1938, most patterns were hand painted on the bisque prior to glazing. Trained by the pottery to produce the brush strokes and techniques to be used for each pattern, local women (and a few men) fashioned the leaves, stems, flowers, scenes, and animals commonly seen in Blue Ridge patterns.

Blue Ridge production methods seldom utilized embossed (raised) or incised (cut) methods to outline the pattern designs as did many of the period's potteries. Often the patterns were painted on the unglazed bisque after an outline of the central object of the pattern had been hand stamped on the object. This helped as a point of reference and to provide some sense of consistency in production. For the most part, painters freehanded the details. Obviously, some variances in the same pattern among various painters and even the same painter occurred at different times. These differences make Blue Ridge China truly distinctive; in fact, each piece is an original work of art.

Southern Potteries had a reputation of accommodating its customers, both large and small. Large order customers were able to command small and large changes in standard Blue Ridge patterns to suit the whims of their purchasing agents. On the other end of the spectrum, Southern would accept orders for as few as one dozen of a single item from small order customers. According to Earl Peterson, a former employee, it was not unusual to have upwards of one thousand of these small orders on hand at any point in time.

By the time World War II broke out, Southern Potteries ranked as one of the largest producers of china in the United States. Production reached its peak in the early 1940s when imports were largely excluded from the domestic marketplace. With over 1,000 employees, approximately half of whom were painters, production reached an estimated 17 million pieces a year during the mid-1940s.

Southern Potteries' work force was completely unionized. Approximately half of the employees at any point in time were painters. According to surviving artisans, the starting wage for painters was 13 1/2 cents an hour in 1941.

By maintaining eleven Blue Ridge showrooms throughout the country from New York's Fifth Avenue to San Francisco, Southern Potteries introduced customers to the varied patterns of the largest hand painted china producer in the country. Additionally, Sears & Roebuck and Montgomery Ward carried Blue Ridge china in their stores and mail-order catalogs. It was not unusual to see Blue Ridge china offered as premiums by retail stores and producers of consumer goods throughout the country.

World War II brought Blue Ridge to its height of popularity, and its end sadly brought it gradually to its demise within twelve years after "VJ-Day." After the war, imports gradually increased until, in the mid-1950s, most American potteries were unable to remain competitive with the lower-priced imports, primarily from Japan. Increasing domestic labor costs and the introduction of plastic dishware added to the difficulties American potteries faced. By the end of 1956, Southern Potteries was down to around 600 employees, many of whom worked only part-time. Southern's board of directors voted to close the pottery in January of 1957. Directors were able to close the doors without resorting to bankruptcy; in fact, stockholders received a final dividend.

After closing in 1957, a number of Blue Ridge painters went to the Cannonsburg and Stetson potteries to complete orders existing at the time Southern Potteries closed its doors. This accounts for some of the similarities often seen in the finished products of the three potteries.

The remaining structure of the original Southern Potteries complex stands abandoned today as a small and haunting reminder of what once was the nation's largest producer of hand painted china. Today, it is an attraction only to the growing numbers of Blue Ridge collectors, who sense that no journey to Erwin is complete without visiting the spot where Blue Ridge china had its origins.

"ERWIN"

A
Development Plan

FOR THE
HOLSTON CORPORATION
AT
ERWIN, TENNESSEE

"Erwin, A Planned Development for the Holston Corporation" (Architect Grosvenor Atterbury)

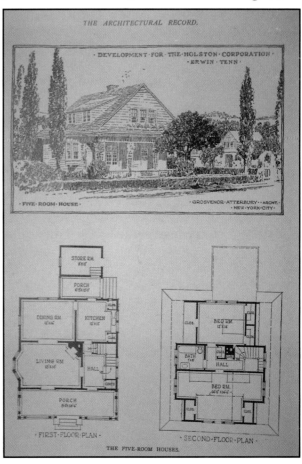

Plan for five-room house designed for pottery workers and their families.

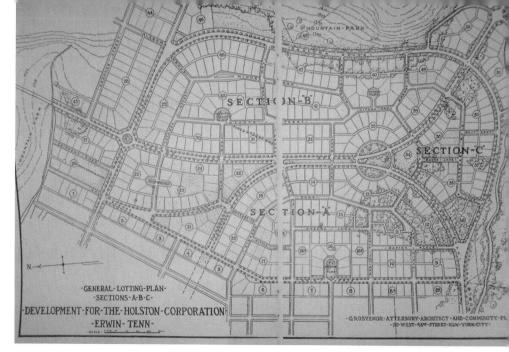

General Lotting Plan by Architect Atterbury.

Hugh W. Kibler, President of Southern Potteries from 1952 through 1957, was elected President of the United States Potters Association in 1953.

Blue Ridge China is featured as centerpiece in 1940s display of products from Tennessee.

Left to right are Webb Gentry, Sales, Albert Price, Sales Manager, and Alvin Miller, Production Supervisor.

Rubber stamp used to list the items to be produced for a particular order by a production line crew.

Rubber stamps were attached to the base of these wooden handles and used to facilitate the stamping of patterns on the bisque.

Rubber stamps were often used to mark the outline of a pattern on the bisque.

Caboose from the CC&O Railroad. The railroad brought the pottery and its earliest workers to Erwin.

Southern Potteries, Erwin, Tennessee.

Chapter 2
Clinchfield China

Many Blue Ridge collectors add Clinchfield China to their collections because it was the genesis for Blue Ridge china. The interest of collectors of early American china in Clinchfield ware, especially BLUEBIRD, has increased its price over the past few years. The advertising market, a large part of pottery production in the early years of the twentieth century, is another area attracting attention in the antique world. Advertising pieces, especially Clinchfield's ROBERT E. LEE AND TRAVELER decal plates and bowls are notably popular. Early Clinchfield production included a variety of shapes, which stayed in production on a lesser scale throughout the years of the pottery.

Southern Potteries produced a limited number of BLUE WILLOW and FLOW BLUE pieces. During our research we were unable to document the exact procedure used to produce the flow blue effect. Employees recalled the paint being sprayed on to the bisque instead of being applied with a brush in the usual manner. Whether or not the chemical, that is normally added to the second glazing process to cause the paint to run or "flow," was used we were unable to determine.

"GOLD WREATH" 7" Pitcher, $75.

"PINK ROSES" Decal, Dinner Plate, $10. Salt and Pepper Shakers, Pair $35.

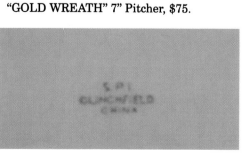

SPI Clinchfield Backstamp on "GOLD WREATH" Pitcher.

"SCONCES" Watauga, Dinner Plate, $25. Creamer, $25. Stamped Clinchfield china decal also used by Salem China.

"DEEP ROSE," Lace Edge, Deep Plate, Marked "#111-26," $20.

MADRIGAL, Lace Edge, 9" Bowl, $20.

Six-sided bottom of "SCONCES" Creamer.

"PAISLEY" 8" Soup Bowl, $20.

"ROSES," Lace Edge, 9" Bowl, $20.

BLUEBIRDS AND BLOSSOMS, Dinner Plate, $30. Saucer, $10. Pendant made from broken plate.

STONE MOUNTAIN, Relief Carving Memorial Plate, $300.

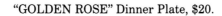

"GOLDEN ROSE" Dinner Plate, $20.

FLOWER BASKET, Watauga, 10" Plate, $25.

"MARIGOLD," Watauga, Bread and Butter Plate, $5.

FLOWER BASKET, Lustre, Scroll Edge, 9" Bowl, $20.

POND IRIS, Platter, $40. Combination transfer and hand painted.

"POPPIES," Watauga, 14" Platter, $25.

Backstamp on POND IRIS Platter, Clinchfield Ware OVEN PROOF, 730.LL.

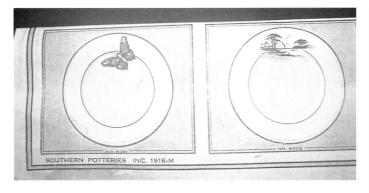

Pattern shown on shipping box: "BUTTERFLY," #6001. "OASIS," #6002.

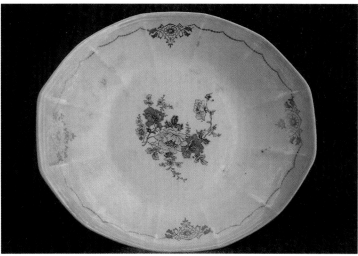

"MARIGOLD," Watauga, Deep Bowl, $30. Often found with "Give us this day our daily bread" inscription.

"GOLD BAND" Cup and Saucer, $10.

Back of "MARIGOLD" Bowl. Inscription: " Compliments of Edward Boehm's Sons General Merchandise Moulton, Texas."

Antique Hand Embroidered Tea Towel.

"MARIGOLD," OES Lustre Plate, $50.

OES Plate, Stamped "Betsy Ross Bread / McGouch Bakeries Corp., / Birmingham, Ala."

OES Commemorative, Lustre, Scroll Edge, Bowl, $50. Inscription: "Grand Chapter of Alabama October 17, 18, 19, 1927, OES, Birmingham, Alabama."

LEWANN, Candlewick Advertising Plate, $40. Inscription: "Hardin Bro. Store of Many Friends Xmas 1940, Watauga Valley, Tenn."

"GOLDEN ROSE," Ashtray, $75.

FLOWER BASKET, Lace Edge, 7" Plate with painted message around border: " Merry Christmas and Happy New Year," $60. Inscription: "Compliments of Herring & Young, Erick, Oklahoma."

"FLOWER," Advertising Ashtray, $60. Inscription: "Compliments of Southern Potteries, Inc., Erwin, Tenn."

Unusual backstamp with Southern Potteries scripted over the Clinchfield Crown.

WILLOWBERRY, Advertising Platter, Candlewick, $50. Inscription: "Compliments of R.E. Grant Irving, VA."

(Left to right) "Clinchfield Railroad Company" 5" Ashtray, $75. Tulip Ashtray, $60. Message: "Max Friedman Jeweller Knoxville, Tenn."

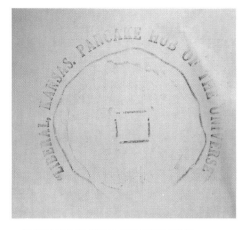

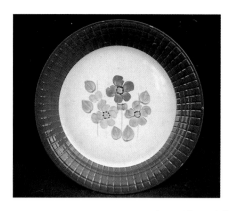

"PANCAKE HUB OF THE UNI-VERSE," Imprint of stamp used for advertising ashtray.

CASSANDRA, Monticello Platter, $20. Also with blue border.

CASSANDRA, Pie Baker, $25. Also with blue border.

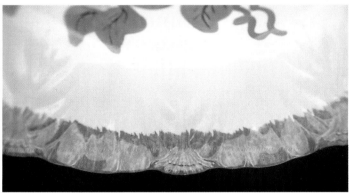

(Top to bottom), TRELLIS, LOTUS LEAF, HONEYCOMB.

(Top to bottom), LACE EDGE, Pitcher and Cup Handles, SCROLL EDGE.

Backstamp on gold border flower decal plates. Popular in their day, decorators and homemakers are again recognizing their charm.

"BURGUNDY CHAIN," Dinner Plate, $25.

6" Salt and Pepper Shakers, Pair $50. Flow blue style with rose decal.

"GOLD CHAIN," Dinner Plate, $25.

"THERESA ROSE," Wide Rib, 9" Bowl, $35. Example of early hand painting.

RED WILLOW, Astor, Dinner Plate, $20. Also found on Colonial shape.

BLUE WILLOW, Trellis, 12" Platter, $50.

"BURGUNDY," Lace Filigree Border, Dinner Plate, $25.

"BLUE BUTTERFLY," Lace Edge, 9" Bowl, $30.

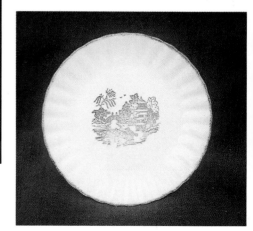

BLUE WILLOW, Colonial, Dinner Plate, $25.

What American collectors have affectionately referred to as "granny bowls," perhaps because we remember them filled with fruit on grandmother's dining room table, seem to have been part of both early and later production at the pottery. Marked with the Clinchfield crown and later Blue Ridge backstamps, they were produced on a variety of shapes including Trellis, Lace Edge, Scroll Edge, and Lotus Leaf. These unique bowls, more often complement, rather than replicate, known patterns. These bowls, also called "nappies" have a sentimental value to many Blue Ridge collectors.

GINGER, Wide Rib, Bowl, $25.

DELICATE, Astor, Bowl, $25. Also found with Lace Edge.

"BLUEBONNETS & POSIES" Bowl, $40. Found on unusual Honeycomb shape.

COURTLAND, Floral Point, Bowl, $30.

RUSSELLVILLE, Scroll Edge, Bowl, $25.

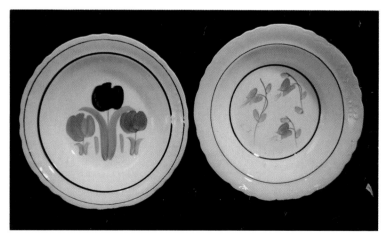

(Left to right) "SILVER TULIPS," Scroll Edge, Bowl, $20. "SILVER HEARTS," Scroll Edge, Bowl $20.

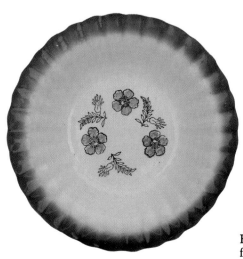

FINESSE, Wide Rib, Bowl, $25. Also found with blue border.

GYPSY FLOWER, Scroll Edge, Bowl, $20. Also found with blue border.

Antique table with Clinchfield and Blue Ridge china.

(Left to right) "RED WINE," Monticello, Bowl, $20. BERRY SPRAY, Scroll Edge, Bowl, $20.

Chapter 3
Floral and Foliage Patterns

The beautiful East Tennessee flowers and stately mountain trees were favorite subjects for Blue Ridge pattern designers. The largest output of dinnerware produced by the pottery was in this genre, many of which appeared on the graceful Colonial shape. Exquisite china accessory pieces, made to match or complement dinnerware sets, were also marketed.

CLINCHFIELD and ASTOR SHAPES

Hand painting was a tentative trial and error process beginning with simple flowers painted around the wide borders of the CLINCHFIELD and ASTOR shapes, progressing to more elaborate designs and culminating in the more fanciful patterns that became characteristic of Blue Ridge dinnerware.

BALSAM POPLAR, Astor, 9" Vegetable Bowl, $30.

FLUFFY RUFFLES, Astor, Dinner Plate, $20.

MAUDE, Astor, Saucer, $5.

BALSAM POPLAR, Candlewick, 9" Vegetable Bowl, $30.

RUBY, Clinchfield, Dinner Plate, $25.

"PORTULACA," Astor, Bread and Butter Plate, $8.

PRIMROSE PATH, Astor, 12" Platter, $30.

Primrose China Backstamp

CUMBERLAND, Astor, Creamer, $20. Soup Bowl, $10.

BEAUTY SECRET, Gravy Boat, $25.

BUG-A-BOO, Astor, Dinner Plate, $15.

ROANOKE, Astor, Tab Bowl, $15. Additional red flower on full pattern.

JESSICA, Astor, Dinner Plate, $20. Also on Colonial shape.

TARA, Astor, Snack Plate without cup, $15. With cup, $25.

SPRING SHOWER, Astor, Dinner Plate, $25.

PAULINE, Astor, Dinner Plate, $15.

CHATELAINE, Astor, Dinner Plate, $40.

WILDLINGS, Astor, Dinner Plate, $15.

BEGGARWEED, Astor, Dinner Plate, $20.

BLOSSOM TIME, Astor, Dinner Plate, $20.

ABBYVILLE, Astor, Square Round Teapot, $125. Sugar with lid, $25. This pattern is also called RED LETTER DAY.

VERONICA, Astor, Dinner Plate, $20.

Linen to coordinate with tulip patterns.

EDITH, Astor, Dinner Plate, $15. Also found with blue edge on Skyline shape.

TUMBLING PETALS, Clinchfield, Dinner Plate, $15.

TULIP ROW, Clinchfield, Dinner Plate, $10.

"BETH'S BEAUTY," Astor, Dinner Plate, $30.

PRICILLA, Clinchfield, Dinner Plate, $20.

PASTEL POPPY, Astor, Dinner Plate, $15.

COLONIAL FAIENCE Backstamp found on "BETH'S BEAUTY" Plate.

24

BOUQUET, Astor, Dinner Plate, $15.

COURTSHIP, Astor, Dinner Plate, $20.

WATERLILY, Astor, Dinner Plate, $15.

"MI + MA" Astor, Cereal Bowl, $10

TRIBUTE, Astor, Bread and Butter Plate, $5. Two flowers found on the full pattern.

ROSEANNA, Astor, Dinner Plate, $15.

CORSAGE, Astor, Cup and Saucer, $15.

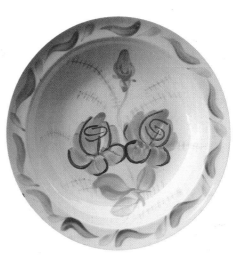

CORSAGE, Astor, Soup Bowl, $20.

SUNDROPS, Ovide, Coffee Pot, $125.

SPRING SONG, Clinchfield, 12" Platter, $25. Also found on Candlewick shape.

BELLEMEADE, Astor, Creamer, $20.

SUNDROPS, Astor, Dinner Plate, $20.

TETE-A-TETE, Astor, 9" Vegetable Bowl, $20.

BELLEMEADE, Astor, Bottom of covered vegetable dish. $30.

COTTON CANDY, Trellis, Plate, $20.

TRIPLET, Astor, Dinner Plate, $10. This plate was advertised as "SUNNYBROOK" in a 1942 Montgomery Ward's catalog. LATTICE FLOWER (VINCA), Cake Lifter, $20.

"DOUBLE DAISY," Astor, Bread and Butter Plate, $5.

CHICKORY, Astor, Bread and Butter Plate, $5. Also on Colonial shape.

WINNER'S CIRCLE, Clinchfield, Dinner Plate, $10.

JONQUIL, Astor, Dinner Plate, $20.

"DODE," Lace Edge, Cereal Bowl, $10.

"TICKLE," Astor, Bread and Butter Plate, $5.

PHYLLIS L. SALAD SET, Astor. (Top) "MIXED BOUQUET" (Middle, Left to right) CROWNVETCH and "BLUE DAISY." (Bottom) "YELLOW DAISY." $20 each. Believed to have been set of eight.

FAIRY TALE, Astor, Soup Bowl, $10.

"RED BOW PLUME," Lace Edge, Butter Pat, $30.

"WHEELIES," Astor, Bread and Butter Plate, $5.

S.P.I. backstamp.

Left: PLUME, Astor, Fruit Bowl, $5. Right: GOLDEN JUBILEE, Astor, Saucer, $5.

MARYLEE, Astor, Dinner Plate, $10. Also found on Colonial and Candlewick shapes.

SALMAGUNDI, Clinchfield, Fruit Bowl, $10.

"REGAL," Scroll Edge, Vegetable Bowl, $25.

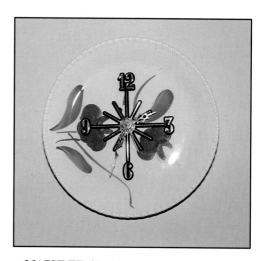

MARYLEE Clock. $25.

PERIWINKLE, Astor, Demi Teapot, $125.
Demi Creamer, $40. Demi Sugar, $40.

PERIWINKLE, Astor, Egg Cup, $30.
Luncheon Plate, $20. Tea Tile, $25. Cup
and Saucer, $25.

PERIWINKLE, Astor, Covered Toast, $120.

Another view of PERIWINKLE covered
toast. This lovely set is referred to as a
Breakfast Set.

COLONIAL SHAPE

This softly fluted shape is as pleasing to today's collectors as it was to the homeowners of the day. Previously successful patterns, were used as a springboard for "fussier" patterns, and equally complex new patterns were also designed. During the pottery's peak years of production, exquisite accessory pieces, including vases, lamps and vanity boxes, were produced in large quantities and a multitude of styles.

DEWBERRY, Dinner Plate, $20.

China cabinet filled with FOX GRAPE dinnerware, one of the most popular Colonial patterns.

ROSE HILL, Dinner Plate, $25.

ROSE HILL, Grace Pitcher, $125.

FOXGRAPE, Dinner Plate, $25.

FLOWER BOWL, Cake Plate, $45.

FLOWER BOWL VARIANT, Cake Plate, $45. Also found in irregular shape.

KAREN, Dinner Plate, $25. Cup, $10.

ERWIN ROSE, Dinner Plate, $25.

ERWIN ROSE, 6 1/2" Virginia Pitcher, $125.

SUNDAY BEST, Dinner Plate, $25.

TIGER LILY, Dinner Plate, $25.

SEREPTA, Dinner Plate, $20.

RAINELLE, Dinner Plate, $25.

ELIZABETH, Dinner Plate, $25.

EXTRAVAGANZA, Dessert Plate, $15.

(Left to right) LAURIE, Saucer, $5. Full pattern has 2 large flowers. LYNNE, Saucer, $5. Also known as GALA AFFAIR.

(Left to right) ANNADEL, Saucer, $5. Full pattern has 6 flowers. RHAPSODY, Saucer, $5.

ROSETTE, Dinner Plate, $15.

BEREA BLOSSOM, 14" Platter, $35.

DRESDEN DOLL, Dinner Plate, $25.

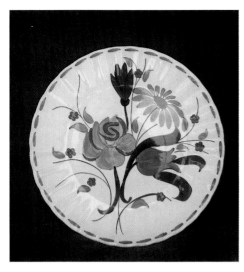

"NEGATHA," Dinner Plate, $30.

Backstamp of "NEGATHA" plate, showing pattern # 3037 with original paper label from pottery. Label reads "Oct. 20, FOB, 32 PC SET."

WILDWOOD FLOWER, Dinner Plate, $25.00.

NADINE, Luncheon Plate, $15.

GARDEN LANE, Cup and Saucer, $15. Bread and Butter Plate, $10. Open Sugar, $20. This pattern was advertised in the Montgomery Ward catalog.

JUNE BOUQUET, Bread and Butter Plate, $10.

(Left to right) DELFT ROSE, Saucer, $5. MEDLEY, Saucer, $5.

ROXALANA, Dinner Plate, $25.

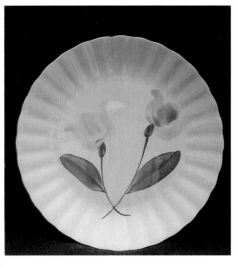

TWOSOME, Dinner Plate, $10.

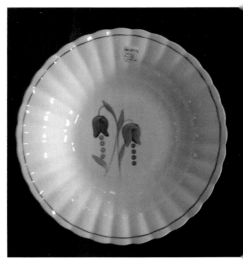

FAIRY BELLS, Vegetable Bowl, $25.

SHOO FLY, Dinner Plate, $15. Open
Sugar and Creamer, $25 set.

TRUE PETUNIA, Sugar with lid, $25.
Blue petunia on other side.

MOUNTAIN BELLS, 12" Platter, $20.

MODESTY, Vegetable Bowl, $20. Also
found with blue border on Candlewick
shape.

PATCHWORK POSY, Cereal Bowl, $10.

PEONY, Cake Plate, $40.

Southern Potteries, Inc. Backstamp also commonly used on Colonial patterns.

WHIRLIGIG, Cup, $8. Bread and Butter, $10. Sometimes found with green edge. Often used in aluminum baskets.

RUTLEDGE, Bread and Butter, $10. Full pattern has 2 tulips. BOW KNOT, color variant of WHIRLIGIG, Cup, $8.

COLONIAL ROSE, Saucer, $10.

RIDGE ROSE, 4" Tile, $40.

RIDGE ROSE, Luncheon Plate, $20. Snack Plate with cup, $35. This pattern was sold by Montgomery Ward catalog.

SPRING HILL TULIP, Cup and Saucer, $15.

"SPRING FIELD," 13" Platter, $25.

CLAIRBORNE, Oval Vegetable Bowl, $25.

"GARDEN DELIGHT", Demi Tray, $50.00.

Backstamp for "GARDEN DELIGHT".

BRIDAL BOUQUET, Cup and Saucer, $20.

MOUNTAIN ASTER, Dessert Plate, $10. Gravy Boat, $25.

CUPID, Dinner Plate, $20.

QUEENIE, Dinner Plate, $20.

SAVANNAH, Dinner Plate, $20.

CHICKORY, Saucer, $5. Sugar with lid, $20.

RUTH ANNA, Creamer, $20. Fruit Bowl, $10. Full pattern shows all flowers from these 2 pieces.

FLUTTER, Dinner Plate, $20. Creamer, $20. Yellow flower on other side of creamer.

WILD ROSE, Sugar with lid, $25.

CYDNEY, Fruit Bowl, $5.

MICKEY, Dinner Plate, $20. Creamer, $20.

RAMBLING ROSE, Cake Plate, $40. Creamer, $25. Gray edge of this pattern distinguishes it from other similar rose patterns.

KIBLER'S ROSE, Dessert Plate, $20. Prickly thorns distinguish this pattern from PAPER ROSES.

LAURA, Bread and Butter, $10. BLACKBERRY LILY, Bread and Butter, $10.

PAPER ROSES, 9" Plate, $15. Cake Lifter, $30. Cake lifter designed to go with many rose patterns.

"ROCK ROSE VARIANT," Cake Plate, $40.

(Left to right) JONQUIL, 7" Square Plate, $25. CAROL'S ROSES, 7" Square Plate, $25. This pattern was often featured in Southern Potteries' ads.

ROSALINDE, Covered Vegetable, $65.

VARIETY, 12" Platter, $20. Flowers curve around plates.

SUN BOUQUET, Cup and Saucer, $15. A 53-piece set could be purchased through Montgomery Ward's catalogue for $19.25.

"SUN BOUQUET VARIANT, " Dinner Plate, $15. Cup, $10.

LOVELY LINDA, Dinner Plate, $15. Plate also found with broken green edge.

VELVET PETALS, Dinner Plate, $20.

EDGEMONT, Dinner Plate, $15.

RADIANCE, Dinner Plate, $15.

"ALLEGANY VARIANT," Dinner Plate, $15.

FLOWER RING, Luncheon Plate, $20.

NORMA, Celery Dish, $20.

TAFFETA, Dinner Plate, $15.

PRAIRIE ROSE, Bread and Butter Plate, $5. Full pattern has 3 flowers around the plate.

GYPSY, Dinner Plate, $15.

ALLEGANY, Dinner Plate, $15.

GYPSY, Creamer, $15. Sugar with lid, $20. BUTTERCUP is an almost identical pattern.

"RED HILL VARIANT," Luncheon Plate, $10. RED HILL does not have a yellow border.

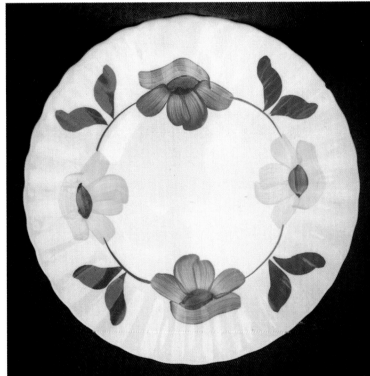

"FRIENDS," Dinner Plate, $15.

SHERRY, Bread and Butter Plate, $5. Full pattern also has a 3-petal blue flower.

NOCTURNE (RED), Dinner Plate, $20.

NOCTURNE (RED), Oversized open
Sugar and Creamer, $45 set.

Courtesy of Lands End.

MIRROR IMAGE, 8" Square Plate, $25.

"RED NOCTURNE VARIANT", Bread
and Butter Plate, $5. Sugar with lid,
$20.

WILD IRISH ROSE (YELLOW), Dinner Plate, $20.

(Left to right) "RED" WILD IRISH ROSE, Butter Pat, $25. DOTTY, Butter Pat, $30. (Bottom) CHINTZ, Butter Pat, $30.

WILD IRISH ROSE (RED),15" Platter, $35.

PEMBROOKE, Dinner Plate, $25.

ORIENTAL POPPY, Dinner Plate, $20.

MOON STRUCK, Vegetable Bowl, $20. Also found with flowers reversed.

POLKA DOT, Creamer, $20.

DREAM FLOWER, Dinner Plate, $25.

FIRST LOVE, Creamer, $15. Saucer, $5.
Also found with flowers reversed.

JOANNA, Soup Bowl, $20.

VIVACIOUS, Bread and Butter Plate,
$5. Also found with flowers reversed.

PLAIN JANE, Dinner Plate, $10.

DUPLICATE, Dinner Plate, $20.

ALLEGRO, Saucer, $5. Also called VI-
BRANT. ALLEGRO, 4" Big Cup, $35.

WINDFLOWER, Creamer, $15. Dinner
Plate, $20.

AMARYLIS, Dinner Plate, $25.

BRIDESMAID, 13" Platter, $20.
Creamer, $15.

CINQUEFOIL, Dinner Plate, $25.

SUSANNAH, Dinner Plate, $25. Some-
times found with flowers reversed and
light green leaves. UCAGO backstamp.
Egg Cup, $25.

CYCLAMEN, Bread and Butter
Plate, $10.

VICTORIA, Dinner Plate, $20. June
Bride Cup, $10. Yellow line on inside of
cup.

BECKY, Range Shaker, $40 set. Dinner
Plate, $20. Cup, $5.

BROOKNEAL, Dinner Plate, $15.

"POPPY," Dinner Plate, $15.

"BOERNE," Dinner Plate, $25.

DEEP PURPLE, 15" Irregular-shaped Cake Plate, $50.

NASCO backstamp on "POPPY" plate.

ZINNIA, Tab Bowl, $20.

RED LETTER DAY, Dinner Plate, $25. Also called ABBYVILLE.

"VANILLA," Dinner Plate, $15.

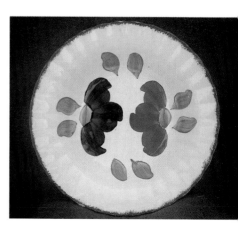

OPPOSITES, Vegetable Bowl, $20.

"HOWDY," Cup and Saucer, $10.

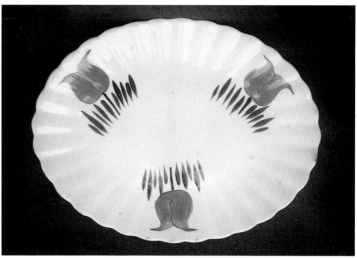

PINE MOUNTAIN TULIP, 10" Platter, $25.

CHERISH, Saucer, $5. Similar pattern on Astor shape is called JOHNSON CITY.

CAROL, Bread and Butter Plate, $5.

DOUBLE DUTCH, Cake Plate, $40.

LOVELY LINDA, Dinner Plate, $10.

"LACY TULIP," Dinner Plate, $15.

TULIP DUO, Saucer, $5. TULIP, Cake Lifter, $25. Cake lifter can be used with many tulip patterns.

RED STITCHES, Saucer, $5.

MARDI GRAS, Square Round Teapot, $125.

"MERRY MARDI GRAS," Dinner Plate, $20.

BERKSHIRE backstamp of RED STITCHES saucer.

MARDI GRAS VARIANT, Dinner Plate, $20. 64-piece set sold for $11.98 in the 1942 Montgomery Ward catalogue.

CHRYSANTHEMUM, 14" Platter, $40. Pattern also called DAHLIA in a 1949 House Beautiful magazine.

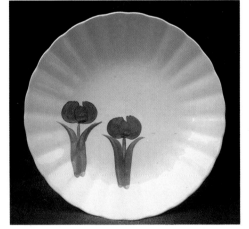

TWO OF A KIND, Cereal Bowl, $8. Marked UCAGO. Similar pattern with different shaped leaves marked Southern Potteries.

MARDI GRAS, Cup and Saucer, $15.

GYPSY DANCER, Bread and Butter Plate, $10. Matching yellow flower is on the full pattern.

MAIDENPINK, Bread and Butter Plate, $5.

CHAMPAGNE PINKS, 15" Platter, $40.

SWEET PEA, Cup, $10. Dinner Plate, $20.

(Left to right) ENDEARING, Bread and Butter Plate, $5. Full pattern has two small buds. CAPTIVATE, Bread and Butter Plate, $5. Full pattern has two flowers. Patterns are very similar.

GARLAND, Egg Cup, $25.

TICKLED PINK, Egg Cup, $25.

OLD REFRAIN, Cup and Saucer, $20.

PETUNIA, Cake Plate, $40. Cake Lifter, $25. Desert Plates, $10.ea. Pattern is stamped LAUREL WREATH.

JOYCE, Bread and Butter Plate, $5. Creamer, $20.

Backstamp for PETUNIA plate, indicating LAUREL WREATH pattern name.

"HEARTSPRIGS," Bread and Butter Plate, $5.

"BARBERRY BOW," Cereal Bowl, $15.

GARDEN GREEN backstamp.

MANASSAS, Cup and Saucer, $25.

GARDEN GREEN, Cup and Saucer, $20.

50

GARDEN GREEN (BLUE), Cake Plate, $45.

(Left to right) DOGTOOTH VIOLET, Blossom Top, Good Housekeeping China Shaker, $100 set. "VIOLET" Dinner Plate, $30. DOGTOOTH VIOLET, China Shaker, $75 set.

AMHURST, Fruit Bowl, $10.

GARDEN GREEN (BLUE), 6 1/2" Ramekin with lid, $50.

Backstamp for "VIOLET" plate: BLUE RIDGE MOUNTAINS HANDART.

Backstamp for VIOLETS FOR JEAN plate.

PRINCESS, Saucer, $5.

GARDEN GREEN (YELLOW), and GARDEN GREEN (RED), 2 1/4" Ramekins with lids, $30 each.

VIOLETS FOR JEAN, Dinner Plate, $30. Note similarity to "VIOLET" plate.

ORLINDIA, Dinner Plate, $15.

SPRING GLORY, Dinner Plate, $20.
Also found on Candlewick shape.

BLUE FLOWER, Dinner Plate, $10.

BAILEY BLUE, Fruit Bowl, $8.

ELNORA, 8" Plate, $10. Saucer has
yellow flower, and cup has the blue
flower.

VERONA, Gravy Boat, $25. Lid for
sugar bowl, $5. Full pattern has an
additional flower.

BLUEFIELD, Dinner Plate, $20. Name
also used for a dissimilar pattern. See
index.

"MAXIE," 13" Platter, $20.

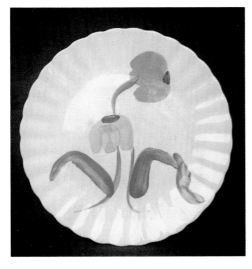
"CONNIE," Dinner Plate, $10. Saucer has blue flower. Cup has yellow flower.

BLUE TANGO, 14" Platter, $40.

BLUE HEAVEN, Dinner Plate, $20.

CROCUS, Dinner Plate, $20.

BARBARA, 5" Antique Pitcher, $120.

COWETA, Dinner Plate, $20.

YELLOW IRIS, Saucer, $5.

BARBARA, Dinner Plate, $25.

DEEP GREEN, Dinner Plate, $20.

PRISTINE, 10 1/2" Salad Bowl, $60. Serving fork and spoon also produced.

VIRGIE, Dinner Plate, $15.

FUCHSIA, Bread and Butter Plate, $10. Vase in this pattern seen on second shelf.

Shelf with favorite patterns.

ORIAN, 9" Oval Celery Dish, $20. Darker shades of this pattern may also be found.

TRIANGLE LINES, Cup, $10. This uncharacteristically modern Colonial pattern has solid blue saucers and plates.

DAYDREAM, Bread and Butter Plate, $5. Full pattern also has bud at top of plate.

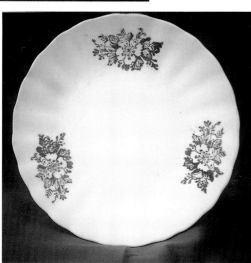

BARWICK, Bread and Butter Plate, $5.

Frosted glasses with SINGLE POINSETTIA and YELLOW MUM patterns from the GARDEN FLOWERS set.

Shelf displaying GARDEN FLOWERS Salad Set. Dennison's ad in *House Beautiful* combines a 4-plate set called SPRING GARDEN and a 4-place set called FINE BLOSSOMS.

IRIS ANN, 8" Plate, $25.

LAVENDER IRIS, 8" Plate, $25.

RED CONE FLOWER, 8" Plate, $25.

FONDEVILLE backstamp found on this popular salad set called FONDEVILLE FLEURS. PURPLE MAJESTY, similar to PURPLE POSY is not shown.

"HYDRANGEA," 8" Plate, $25. From the FONDEVILLE FLEURS set.

"CAMELLIA," 8" Plate, $25. From the FONDEVILLE FLEURS set.

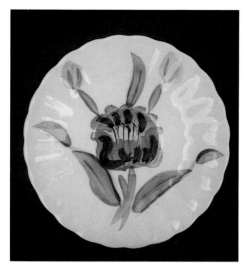

TAZEWELL TULIP, Saucer, $10. Flowers repeated on full pattern.

KING'S RANSOM, Saucer, $8. Shaggy leaves distinguish this pattern from WRINKLED ROSE pattern.

WRINKLED ROSE, (yellow edge), Dinner Plate, $20. Cake Lifter, $25.

DWARF IRIS, Dinner Plate, $25.

WRINKLED ROSE, (yellow edge), Cup and Saucer, $25.

"OCTOBER," 4-Piece Place Setting, $40.

(Left to right) WRINKLED ROSE, (pink edge), Bread and Butter Plate, $5. WRINKLED ROSE, (gray basketweave), Bread and Butter Plate, $10.

SYMPHONY, Dinner Plate, $20. Demi Sugar, $50.

LOUISA, Dinner Plate, $10. Also found on Piecrust Shape.

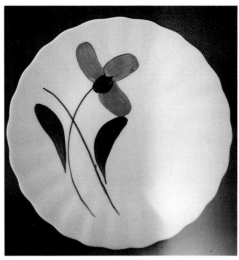

MERRIMENT, Bread and Butter Plate, $5. Two flowers on full pattern. Also found on Candlewick shape.

CHATAM, Bread and Butter Plate, $5. Barrel Shaker, $20 set.

MARYLEE, Dinner Plate, $10. Also found on Clinchfield and Candlewick shapes.

MOD TULIP, Dinner Plate, $10.

TESS, Bread and Butter Plate, $5.

KISMET, Dinner Plate, $10.

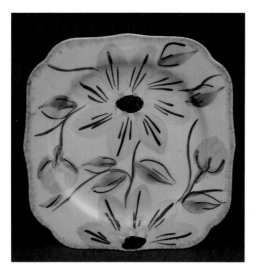

SUNFIRE, (GRAY), 8" Square Plate, $25.

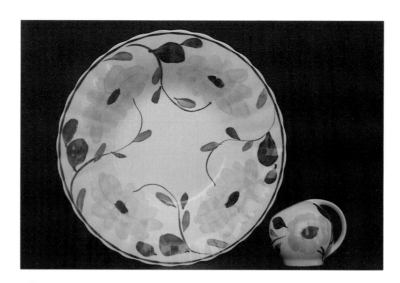

SUNBRIGHT, Vegetable Bowl, $20.
DAISY GOLD, Shaker, $25 set.

SUNFIRE, (TEAL), 14" Platter, $40.

RUGOSA, 12" Cake Plate, $40. Sanka advertised RUGOSA in Life magazine, 1947.

DAZZLE, Dinner Plate, $10.

VIRGINIA GOLD, Dinner Plate, $15.

"JUDY," Dinner Plate, $15.

"MYRLEEN," Bottom of Covered Vegetable, $30 bottom only. Note rim to accommodate lid.

EARLY BLOSSOM, Dinner Plate, $10.

DELTA DAISY, Two-Tier Tidbit, $25.

CYNTHIANA, Dinner Plate, $15. Egg Cup, $35. Children's sets have been found in this pattern.

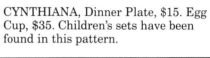

YELLOW PETUNIA, Salad Set, $150 set.

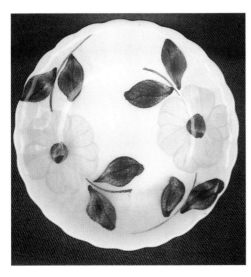

DELTA DAISY, Fruit Bowl, $5.

MOUNTAIN DAISY, Dinner Plate, $10.

HORNBEAK, Dinner Plate, $10.

SPIDERWORT, Cup and Saucer, $20.

SUNFLOWER, Teapot, $100.

"PATSY," Saucer, $5. Blue dots differentiate this pattern from LIGHT HEARTED.

COREOPSIS, Dinner Plate, $15. There is also a LACE LEAF COREOPSIS.

MIRROR, MIRROR, Saucer, $5. Full pattern has 3 flowers in a triangular design.

LIGHTHEARTED, Dinner Plate, $15. Cup, $5.

CELANDINE, Dinner Plate, $15. Demi Creamer, $40.

SUNNY, Dinner Plate, $15.

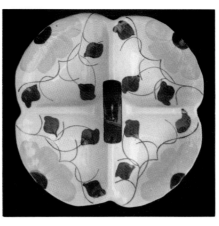

HALF & HALF, Center Handle Four Section Relish, $65.

TALLAHASSEE, Dinner Plate, $10. Cup, $5.

TRIPLE TREAT, Dinner Plate, $15.

RIDGE DAISY, Creamer, $20. Sugar with lid, $25. Square Box in HALF & HALF pattern, $50. Several "daisy" patterns mix well.

YELLOW NOCTURNE, 17" Platter, $60. Yellow line around edge distinguished this pattern from RIDGE DAISY.

NIOTA, 12" Platter, $20. Small pieces only have 1 flower.

"YELLOW GAIETY," Bread and Butter Plate, $8. Found in red as well.

"SUNNY UP," Dinner Plate, $10.

COUNTRY ROAD VARIANT, Dinner Plate, $15.

(Left to right) LOVELY, Saucer, $5. COUNTRY ROAD, Bread and Butter Plate, $5. Full pattern has 2 more flowers.

DESERT SPRING, Bread and Butter Plate, $5. Cup, $5. Also found on Skyline shape.

STRATHMOOR, Barrel Shaker, $25 set. Bread and Butter Plate, $5.

Backstamp most often used on Colonial pieces.

FIELD DAISY, 13" Platter, $40.

FIELD DAISY, Butter Dish, $50.

ANGELINA, Sugar with lid, $25. Dinner Plate, $30.

AUTUMN BERRY, Bread and Butter Plate, $10. 6" Bowl, $20.

AUTUMN LAUREL, Saucer, $5. Also advertised in Montgomery Ward's catalogue.

MEMPHIS, China Shaker, $75 set. Marked #975-4

MEMPHIS, Fruit Bowl, $8.

ROSE MARIE, Chocolate Pot, $200. Pedestal Sugar and Creamer, Each $50. This chocolate pot was featured in a Geneva Kitchen ad in 1953 Saturday Evening Post.

GRANDMOTHER'S GARDEN, Colonial, Gravy Boat, $30.

CALICO, Pedestal Sugar and Creamer, Each $40.

ROSE MARIE, Ovide Coffee Pot, $125.

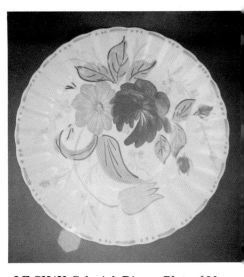

ROSE MARIE, Colonial, Saucer, $10.

WALTZ TIME, Colonial, Dinner Plate, $30.

LE SHAY, Colonial, Dinner Plate, $30.

Imagine a very large tray containing all the beautiful flowers, multicolored leaves, and flowing stems of all the dash-dot-dot-dot edged patterns. This picture in our minds helps to explain the similarity of these cherished patterns. Because of the deep resemblance, with no one distinguishing characteristic such as the pink flower of ROSE MARIE or the two shaded ones of ELEGANCE, we have called NOVE ROSE and VERNA the "sister" patterns. It is interesting to note that these patterns strongly resemble French, English and Italian styles popular before and after the war, especially an Italian pattern called, what else, NOVE ROSE.

VERNA, Maple Leaf Relish, $60. NOVE ROSE, China Shakers, Pair $90.

NOVE ROSE, Square Box, $100. Ashtray, $20.

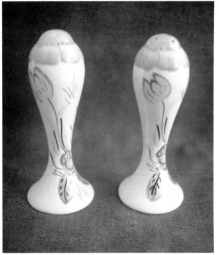

NOVE ROSE, Blossom Top Shakers, Pair $100.

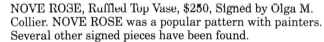

NOVE ROSE, Ruffled Top Vase, $250, Signed by Olga M. Collier. NOVE ROSE was a popular pattern with painters. Several other signed pieces have been found.

NOVE ROSE, Colonial, Saucer, $10. Bread and Butter Plate, $15. Previously, Nove Rose was thought to be only an accessory pattern. Presence of dinnerware pieces confirms that it was a complete line.

NOVE ROSE, Fine Panel Teapot, $150.

ROMANCE, Chocolate Pot, $250. Reverse.

NORA, Flared Creamer, $75.

ROMANCE, Chocolate Pot, $250.

ROMANCE, Gold Trimmed Pedestal Creamer and Sugar, Each $90.

ROMANCE, Chocolate Set Tray, $600.

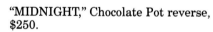

"MIDNIGHT," Chocolate Pot, $250.

"MIDNIGHT," Chocolate Pot reverse, $250.

SPRING BOUQUET, Flared Sugar, $50.

"MIDNIGHT," Chocolate Pot Set, $900.

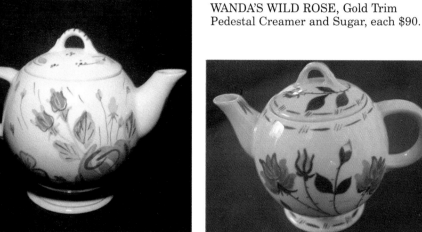

Petite, 4 1/4" Mini Ball Teapots are infrequently seen.

WANDA'S WILD ROSE, Gold Trim Pedestal Creamer and Sugar, each $90.

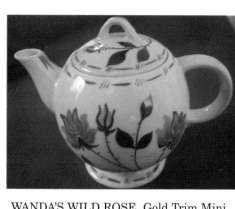

DOGTOOTH VIOLET, Mini Ball Teapot, $175.

"JETTA," Mini Ball Teapot, $200.

WANDA'S WILD ROSE, Gold Trim Mini Ball Teapot, $250.

TUCKER, Mini Ball Teapot, $150.

6 1/4" Snub Nose Teapot, $100.

ROSE BOUQUET, Snub Nose Teapot, $100. Marked "#13/2."

Bottom of Snub Nose Teapot

CASTLEWOOD, Chevron Handle Teapot, $125.

LORRAINE, Fine Panel Teapot, $100. Coordinates well with ANNALEE pattern.

GALORE, Clara Pitcher, $75. Marked "Clara Jug Dec. #1."

YELLOW ROSE, Chevron Handle Teapot, $150.

ELEGANCE, Virginia Pitcher, 6 1/2", $150. ELEGANCE contains many of the NOVE ROSE and VERNA flowers.

Clara shape pitcher in flow blue style, stamped "Made in Czechoslovakia." Because of the almost identical shape, these pitchers have been mistakenly attributed to Blue Ridge.

ELEGANCE, Virginia Pitcher, 6 1/2", Reverse, $150. Blue Ridge China Backstamp with "Virginia."

HAPPILY EVER AFTER, Fine Panel Teapot, $125. Similar to WANDA's WILD ROSE.

WHIG ROSE, Rebecca Pitcher, $175.

IDA ROSE, Sally Pitcher, $150.

EUNICE, Watauga Pitcher, 5 1/4", $275.

EUNICE, Reverse of Watauga Pitcher, 5 1/4", $275.

"LADY", Grace Pitcher, $125. Stamped "Grace Jug #1."

PALACE, Milady Pitcher, $175.

PALACE, Milady Pitcher, Reverse, $175.

SUWANEE, Grace Pitcher, 5 1/2", $125. Blue Ridge China stamped "Grace."

EASTER PARADE, Milady Pitcher, 8 1/2", $175.

ANNIVERSARY SONG, Virginia Pitcher, 4 1/4", $100.
PAINTED DAISY, Virginia Pitcher, 4 1/4", $125. Virginia
Pitchers were also made in a 6 1/2" size.

ROSE OF SHARON, Helen Pitcher, $175. China Shakers,
Set $95.

PARTY GOER, Virginia Pitcher, 6 1/2",
$125. Stamped "Virginia Jug #1." BIG
BLOSSOM, Grace Pitcher, $100.

"SEA MIST," Helen Pitcher, $200.
"White Sands," Spiral Pitcher, 7", $150.

TRALEE ROSE, Spiral Pitcher, 4 1/2",
$150.

MILLIE'S PRIDE, Virginia Pitcher, 6 1/
2", $85.

SCATTER, Jane Pitcher, $95

PANSY TRIO, Spiral Pitcher, 7", $85.

70

ANNIVERSARY SONG, Spiral Pitcher, 4 1/2", $125.

SERENADE, Leaf Celery, $75. Spiral Pitcher, 4 1/2", $125.

CHINTZ, Helen Pitcher, $95.

HAZEL, Candy Box Lid, $125. CHINTZ, Candy Box Bottom, $100. CHINTZ, Pedestal Sugar, $50.

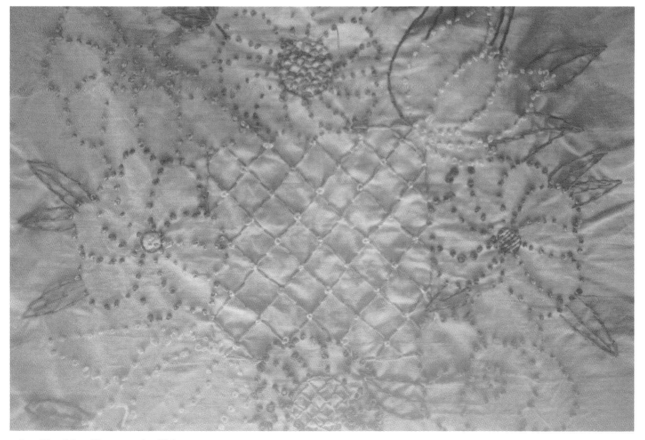

Candlewick pillowcase in Chintz pattern.

Antique china pitchers were made in 3 1/2" and 5" sizes. Six inch Antique shape is called Alice.

PIXIE, Flat Shell Bon-Bon, $125.

"GINNY," Antique Pitcher, 3 1/2", $175.

OPULENCE, Alice Pitcher, 6", $175.

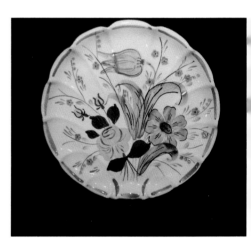

EVALINA, Flat Shell Bon-Bon, $100. Stamped "Dorothy Bon-Bon #1."

ROMANCE, Antique Pitcher, 5", $125. ANNETTE'S WILD ROSE, Antique Pitcher, 5", $125.

PALACE, Flat Shell Bon-Bon, $125. Thought to have been given away to patrons of the Palace Theater in Erwin.

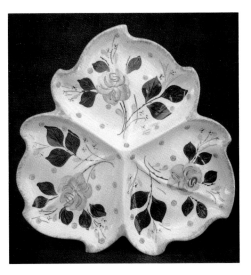

"ENGLISH ROSE," Martha Snack Tray, $175. Blue Ridge China backstamp with "DEC. #3."

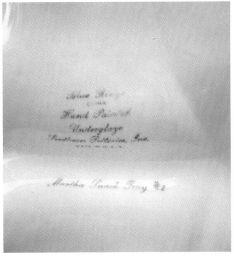

Blue Ridge China backstamp inscribed " Martha Snack Tray #2."

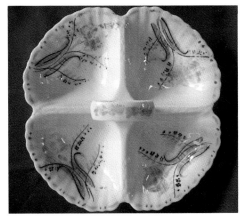

IRIS, Center Handle Dish with Four Sections, $90.

ROSE PARADE, Martha Snack Tray, $150.

BUTTONS & FORGET-ME-KNOTS, Heart Relish, $55.

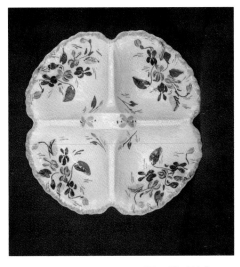

"VERY VIOLET," Center Handle Dish with Four Sections, $100.

IRRESISTABLE, Martha Snack Tray, $150.

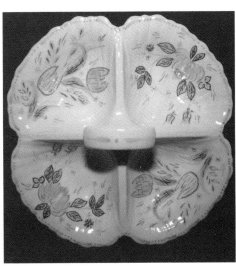

NOVE ROSE, Center Handle Dish with Four Sections, $80.

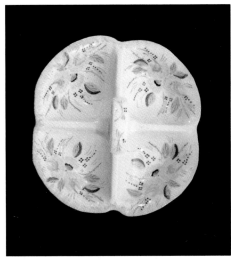

ELLEN, Center Handle Dish with Four Sections, $60.

SERENADE, Center Handle Dish with Four Sections, $70.

"NASCO VIOLETS," Deep Shell, $90. Stamped "NASCO Shell Bon-Bon #2."

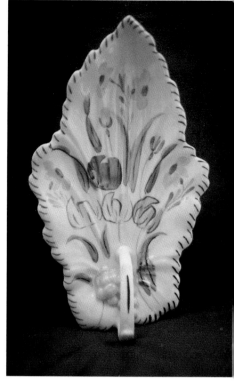

EASTER PARADE, Leaf Celery, $75.

BELVEDERE, Deep Shell, $70. Stamped "Shell Bon-Bon #3." Also found in teal.

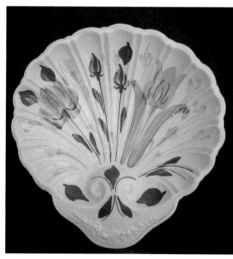

"CHERYL'S GARDEN," Deep Shell, $80. Stamped 'Shell DEC. #4."

RIDGE ROSE, Deep Shell, $90.

SUMMERTIME, Leaf Celery, $65. Leaf Celeries are approximately 10 1/2" x 6 1/4."

TUSSIE MUSSIE, Maple Leaf Relish, $95.

MELODY, Maple Leaf Relish, $85.

ANNIVERSARY SONG, Maple Leaf Relish, $85.

TAHITIAN BLOSSOMS, Loop Handle Relish, 12", $75.

MILLIE'S PRIDE, Maple Leaf Relish, $85.

"RENE & DANNY," Mod Leaf Relish, 10 3/4", $85.

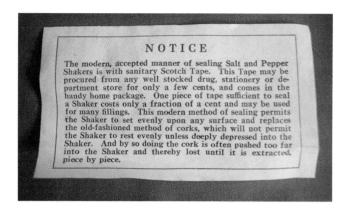

Notice packed with salt and pepper shakers.

"NOVA LEDA," China Shakers, Pair $75. "Ruff Rose", Pair $75.

(Left to right) SWEET SUE, China Shakers, Pair $75. ROSE OF SHARON, China Shakers, Pair $75.

(Left to right) PAINTED DAISY, China Shakers, Pair $75. WRINKLED ROSE, China Shakers, Pair $75.

(Left to right) GARDEN LANE, China Shakers, Pair $75. TARA, China Shakers, Pair $75.

(Left to right) KIBLER'S ROSE, China Shakers, Pair $75. CALICO, China Shakers, Pair $75.

CHARM HOUSE, Pitcher with red leaves, $250.

CHARM HOUSE, Shakers, Pair $125.

CHARM HOUSE, Ramekin, $150.

CHARM HOUSE, Backstamp on Ramekin base. These embossed pieces were made for a New York China Distributor in the late forties.

BUD TOP SHAKERS with gold trim, Pair $100.

CHARM HOUSE, Bud Top Shakers with yellow flower, Pair $175. These embossed CHARM HOUSE shakers are unusual because the pattern is also very similar to GOOD HOUSEKEEPING ROSE.

HAMPTON, Bulbous Vase with embossed flower, 5 1/4", $95.

CHARM HOUSE, Pitcher with green leaves, $250.

HAMPTON, Bottom of bulbous vase. This vase is another embossed pattern, which have been produced for Charm House.

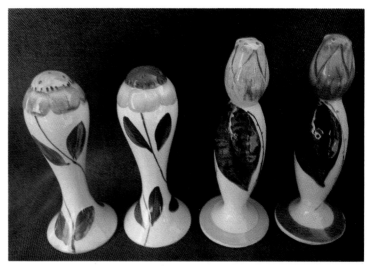

BLOSSOM TOP SHAKERS, 5 1/4", Pair $100. The salt is yellow and the pepper is rose. Sometimes marked "#420. BUD TOP SHAKERS, 5 3/4", Pair $100.

77

GOOD HOUSEKEEPING ROSE,
Creamer and Sugar, Set $75.

GOOD HOUSEKEEPING ROSE, Salt
and Pepper Shakers, Pair $125. Top of
pepper shaker is green.

Backstamp used on Good Housekeeping
items.

GOOD HOUSEKEEPING ROSE, Teapot, $150.

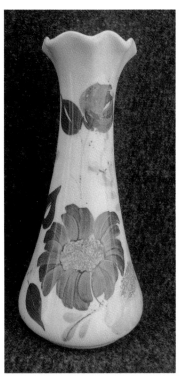

MELODY, Ruffle Top Vase, 9", $85. Has Blue Ridge China
stamp with "#30."

FLO, Ruffle Top Vase, 9", $85. Has Blue Ridge China stamp
with "500/1."

"HELEN," Bud Vase, $150.

"LISA," Bud Vase, 5", $150.

"NELDA," Bud Vase, $150.

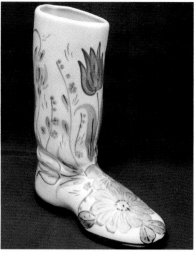

SUMMERTIME, Boot Vase, 8", $85.

MOOD INDIGO, Tapered vase, 7 1/4", $90.

GLADYS, Boot Vase, 8", $85.

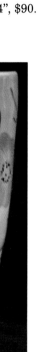

SUMMERTIME, Reverse of Boot Vase, 8", $85. Boot has brown sole. Sometimes the dot-dash border varies in shades of blue.

GLADYS, Reverse of Boot Vase, 8", $85. Boot vases are seldom marked.

GLADYS, Boot Vase with gold trim, 8", $100.

"ANNA," Grecian Style Lamp, $200. Made for American Home. Measures 11" x 4 1/2."

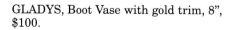

"ELEGANT ROSE," Handled Vase, $200. One view of pitcher shows ELEGANCE-like pattern, and other side resembles NOVE ROSE.

Backstamp for 7 1/4" Handled Vases "Genuine Porcelain, Vanity Fair."

"ANN," Handled Lamp, $125.

ELEGANT ROSE, Reverse of vase.

Close up photograph of vase top, which has been altered to hold the lamp shaft.

ROSE OF SHARON, Handled Vase, $105.

GOOD HOUSEKEEPING stamp also used on handled vases.

(Left to right) TAFOYA TULIP, Handled Vase, $85. MUM SPRAY, Handled Vase, $95. STEPHANIE, Handled Vase, $105.

"PENNINGTON," Lamp made from Handled Vase, $200.

"BETH'S LILY," Candy Box, $400. Rare candy box decorated with lily.

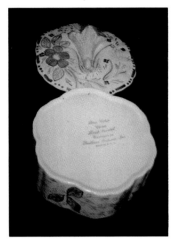

"BRYAN & KIM," Lamp made from Handled Vase, $200.

'BETH'S LILY,' Backstamp and lid. Boxes are hexagonal shaped measuring 5 3/4' x 3 1/4."

"ELUSIVE," Round Vanity Box, $150. Measures 4 3/4" x 1 3/4.

ANIVERSARY SONG, Sherman Lily Box, $350. Spoon Rest, $6.

DOGTOOTH VIOLET, Candy Box, $200.

"PEARL," Rose Step Box, $250. This box has a soft iridescent mother-of-pearl finish.

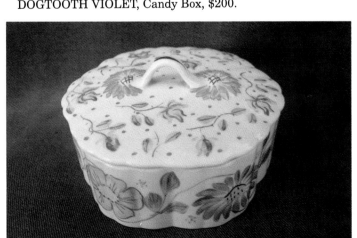

TANGLEWOOD, Candy Box Lid, $100. KATHERINE, Candy Box Base, $75.

ROSE STEP BOX, $200. Measures 4" x 5 1/2'x 4".

DANCING NUDE BOX, $300. Hexagonal shape with wreaths on alternating sides. Measures 2 3/8"x3 1/2.". The nude figure on the lid is in relief.

"SISTERS," Square Box, $50.

"POWDER PUFFS," Square Box, $50.

SEASIDE BOX, $200. Measures 4 1/2" x 3 1/4." Box is sculptured and footed.

BUTTERFLY, Square Box, $100.

CALICO, Square Box, $50.

VIOLET CIRCLE, Square Box, $100. GAILEY, Ashtray, $20. Ashtrays are approximately 3'x3."

SERENADE, Square Box, $50.

Blue Ridge box used for packing square china boxes. EASTER PARADE, Square Box, $90.

DIAMOND DUST, Square Box, $50, Ashtray, $20.

WILD IRISH ROSE, Square Box, $50, Ashtray, $20.

Betsy Jugs (Pitchers) were made in earthenware and in china and were not always marked. They are found in a number of colors and patterns and measure 9" x 3 1/2".

"BLUE FLOWER," Betsy Jug, $85.
"YELLOW FLOWER," Betsy Jug, $85.

Blue Ridge Betsy's have well-defined hands and fingers.

TULIP BETSY, Betsy Jug, $125.

BRICK BETSY, Betsy Jug, $125.

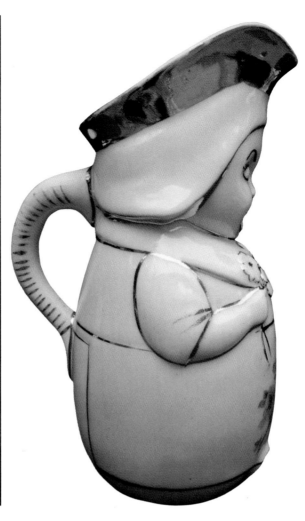

"CHARCOAL BETSY,"
Betsy Jug, $85.

"GOLD BETSY," Betsy Jug, $250.

Side view of GOLD BETSY.

(Left to right) "ROSE FLOWER," Betsy
Jug, $85. "GREEN FLOWER," Betsy Jug,
$75. "RED FLOWER," Betsy Jug, $85.

"FLOW," Betsy Jug, $75. A flow blue look
on an earthenware Betsy Jug.

CANDLEWICK SHAPE

Beaded edges have always given a regal look to dinnerware. Blue Ridge CANDLEWICK Patterns, which often bear the SPI backstamp, range from ornate border designs to soft, elegant flowery bouquets. Many patterns are favorites of Blue Ridge collectors.

COUNTRY GARDEN, Bread and Butter Plate, $10.

(Left to right) "HYDRANGEA," Colonial, Salad Plate, $25. From the FONDEVILLE FLEURS SALAD SET. "HYDRANGEA," Candlewick, Salad Plate, $25.

HIGHLAND POSY, Bread and Butter Plate, $10.

HIGHLAND POSY Backstamp.

PEONY BOUQUET, 13" Platter, $20. Platters were seldom backstamped.

FULL BLOOM, Dinner Plate, $20.

FORGET-ME-NOT, Bread and Butter Plate, $10.

"MASCARA," Tea Tile, $25.

UCAGO Plate as found. See next photograph.

UCAGO backstamp for "ANDREA" and "LEIGH" plates.

SHELLFLOWER, Dinner Plate, $20.

"ANDREA," Dinner Plate, $15. UCAGO plate after washing.

FLOWER WREATH, Ovide Coffee Pot, $125.

FLOWER WREATH, Bread and Butter Plate, $10.

"LEIGH," Dinner Plate, $15.

SWEET PEA VARIANT, Saucer, $5. Full pattern has six flowers. SWEET PEA, Dinner Plate, $20.

SEAROSE VARIANT, Bread and Butter Plate, $5.

GLAMOUR, Salad Fork and Spoon, Set $70.

JAN, Cake Plate, $45.

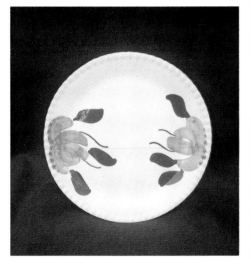

SEAROSE, Bread and Butter Plate, $5. Also found in Colonial.

Mount Vernon backstamp on MARDI GRAS pattern.

TROUSSEAU, Dinner Plate, $25.

GLAMOUR, Cup and Saucer, $20.

MARDI GRAS, Dinner Plate, $20. Creamer, $20.

ROSEBUDS, Dinner Plate, $20. Cup, $10.

SWEET CLOVER, Tab Fruit Bowl, $10. Dinner Plate, $15.

ROSEBUDS backstamp.

TRIBUTE, Dinner Plate, $20.

BLEEDING HEART, Dinner Plate, $25.

"SWEETLY," Cup, $5. Dinner Plate, $20.

POPPY DUET, 13" Platter, $25. Yellow poppy on saucers; red poppy on cups.

"ROBERT," Square Tile, $30. Tiles are seldom marked.

"DANA'S GARDEN," Dinner Plate, $15.

"SPRING FIELD," Dinner Plate, $20.

PURPLE POSY, 13" Platter, $20.
PURPLE POSY, Colonial, Cup and
Saucer, $15.

BLUE MIST, 14" Platter, $40.

TILLIE, Cup, $5. TILLIE, Colonial,
Saucer, $5.

"BLUE ROSE," Dinner Plate, $15.

89

BLUE MOON, Dinner Plate, $25.

"SHY ROSE", Square Tile, $20.

BLUEBELL BOUQUET (Green Leaf),
Ball Teapot, $125.

"OAKCREEK DOGWOOD," Fruit Bowl,
$5.

BLUEBELL BOUQUET (Green Leaf), 3
1/2" x 3 1/4" Egg Cup, $30. 6" Square
Plate, $30.

GLORIOUS, Dinner Plate, $20.

BLUEBELL BOUQUET (Yellow Leaf),
Dinner Plate, $25. Salad Spoon and
Fork, Set $70.

CARNIVAL, Dinner Plate, $20.

Stenciled tablecloth resembling FIRE-CRACKER pattern.

MOUNTAIN NOSEGAY, Dinner Plate, $25. Creamer, $20. Sugar, $25. This pattern with green line is called BEAUTY SECRET.

FIRECRACKER, Bread and Butter Plate, $10.

RUTLEDGE, Vegetable Bowl, $25. Variation of this pattern is found on Colonial.

HARMONY, Cereal Bowl $10.

MAYDAY, Vegetable Bowl, $20.

TRIFLE, Vegetable Bowl, $20.

GUMDROP TREE, Dinner Plate, $15. UCAGO backstamp. Children's sets have been found in this pattern.

ROSEMARY, Cup and Saucer, $25. Also called TULIP RING.

MULTICOLOR TULIP TRIO, Dinner Plate, $20. Many color variations were produced.

"JEAN," Bread and Butter Plate, $5.

DUTCH TULIP, Dinner Plate, $15.

TULIP TIME, Luncheon Plate, $15.

DUTCH BOUQUET, Bread and Butter Plate, $5.

GRASS FLOWER Fruit Bowl $5.

MAGIC FLOWER, 12" Platter, $25.

POM POM, Dinner Plate, $20. Blue flower on saucer, red on cup. "POM POM VARIANT," Patterns without red line found on Colonial shape.

ALLEGRO, 12" Platter, $30. Also called VIBRANT.

SUNDOWNER, Dinner Plate, $20.

AMELIA, Fruit Bowl, $5.

RED HILL, Dinner Plate, $20. RED HILL found on Colonial shape with light green leaves.

SPRING GLORY, Dinner Plate, $20. Also found on Colonial shape.

MOUNTAIN ROSE, Bread and Butter Plate, $5.

MOUNTAIN ROSE backstamp.

CRIMSON TRIO, Dinner Plate, $20.

TWIN FLOWERS, Vegetable Bowl, $25.

SHOWGIRL, 7" Square Plate, $20.

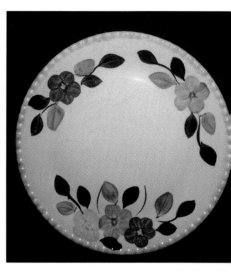

CONFETTI, Dinner Plate, $20.

BETTY, Cup and Saucer, $25. Full pattern has both flowers.

DUTCH IRIS, Dinner Plate, $15. Cup, $5.

BRAMBLE, Skyline, Cup, $5. Sugar with lid, $20.

BRUNSWICK, Dinner Plate, $15.

VIXEN, Bread and Butter Plate, $5. Dinner plate has an additional flower, the color of the edge.

MOUNTAIN IVY, Creamer, $20. Dinner Plate, $20. Similar to, but not as popular as, FOX GRAPE.

STARFLOWER, Ashtray, $25. Possibly an advertising piece.

"GWEN," 13" Platter, $35.

STARFLOWER, Two Tier Tidbit, $35.

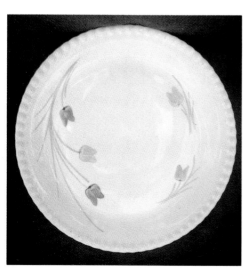

"TINY TULIPS," Dinner Plate, $15.

"ORNAMENTAL," Vegetable Bowl, $25.

RICHARD, Dinner Plate, $20.

SUNSHINE, 13" Platter, $25.

SUNDANCE, Dinner Plate, $20.

"EARLY BLOSSOM VARIANT," 13" Platter, $25.

SUNSHINE VARIANT, Dinner Plate, $20. Backstamp has SUNSHINE name.

ANNABELL, Vegetable Bowl, $25.

EARLY BLOSSOM, Dinner Plate, $15.

ALICIA, Dinner Plate, $15. Also called MOUNTAIN MEADOWS.

YELLOW POPPY, Dinner Plate, $15.

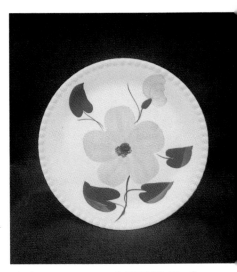

GRANDMOTHER'S PRIDE, Fruit Bowl, $5.

SUNGOLD #1, Dinner Plate, $15.

THINK PINK, Fruit Bowl, $5.

TRIPLET, Covered Toast, Lid Only, $40.
Cake Lifter, $25.

HILDA, 13" Platter, $25.

Salad Servers, (left to right) UPSTART, YELLOW ROSE, PINK PETTICOAT, BORDER PRINT, Each $35. Servers are compatible with more than one pattern.

SPINDRIFT, Tab Bowl, $25.

Colorful assortment of popular patterns.

THE LANGUAGE OF FLOWERS,
These plates have turned Blue Ridge collectors' hearts and budgets "Topsy-Turvy." Translation Courtesy of Jane Greig, Austin American Statesman, and Linda Beamer, Austin Translation and Interpreters Association.

Do you love me a little?

I am not so quick to trust.

l adore you!

You have turned my heart Topsy-Turvy!

You are conquered!

Do you really love me?

Do you really love me?

Will you come with me to the ball?

It is all over!

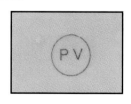

"LANGUAGE OF FLOWERS" plates, $100., each. These plates were also made for PV. A French pottery marketed an almost identical set.

PIECRUST SHAPE

This appropriately named shape, first appearing in the late 1940s, is easily recognized by its crimped edge. Its bright patterns spread themselves lavishly over each piece. Unfortunately too few patterns, new or repeated, have been found.

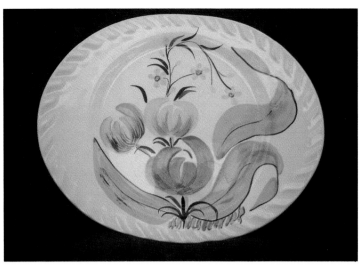

CAMELOT, 13" Platter, $40.

SOUTHERN CAMELLIA, Cup and Saucer, $30. Southern Pottery advertised this pattern in *House Beautiful* magazine in 1948.

SPRING BLOSSOM, Covered Vegetable, $60. Dinner Plate, $25.

JESSAMINE, Tab Bowl $20.

SPRING BLOSSOM, Creamer, $20. Also called CLINCH MOUNTAIN DOGWOOD.

HIGHLAND IVY, Dinner Plate, $20.

MAGNOLIA, Dinner Plate, $25.

BETTY MAE, Fruit Bowl, $5.

99

Juice and water glasses to match Blue Ridge patterns were made by several glass companies. This unidentified glass differs slightly from ones made by Federal.

These matching glasses are attributed to Federal Glass Company.

SOUTHERN SPECIAL, Dinner Plate, $20.

ECHOTA, Dinner Plate, $15. Also found on Colonial shape.

FLORIBUNDA, Dinner Plate, $20.

SECRET GARDEN, Saucer, $5. Full pattern has another flower spray.

DAFFODIL, Creamer, $20. Cup and Saucer, $25.

100

Sunflower tablecloth and juice glass matching several Blue Ridge patterns of the 50's.

"DAYLILY," Covered Vegetable. $60.

FREEDOM, Creamer, $20. Dinner Plate, $15.

TEAL ROSEANNA, Demi Cup and Saucer, $30. Dinner Plate, $20. Egg Cup, $30.

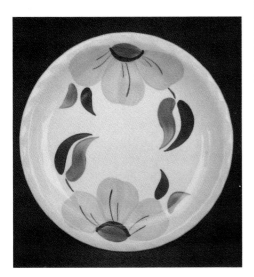

"PEEPERS," Bread and Butter Plate, $5.

SWEET CLOVER, Clock, $25. Some collectors enjoy finding or making clocks to match their favorite pattern.

BOURBON ROSE, Bread and Butter, $5. Full pattern has 2 roses. Also on Colonial shape.

ROSE CAMELLLA, Cup, $10.

FLIRT, Dinner Plate, $20.

ANEMONE, Dinner Plate, $15.

WHIRLIGIG, Dinner Plate, $20.

RED RING, Dinner Plate, $20.

"VIVIAN," Dinner Plate, $20. This pattern is similar to Red Hill.

RING-0-ROSES, Dinner Plate, $20.

CANTATA, Dinner Plate, $15.

MIRROR IMAGE, Dinner Plate, $20.

ARAGON, Dinner Plate, $15.

SAMPLER, Saucer, $5. Not a typical Piecrust pattern.

PLUM NELLY, 6" Square Plate, $20. Full pattern has an additional red flower.

GREEN BRIAR, Creamer, $20. Celery Dish $15.

CADENZA, Gravy Boat, $20.

CANDACE, Square Plate, $20.

CANDACE, 13" Bowl $45.

Back view of CANDACE, probably part of a set of mixing bowls.

A collection of square plates creates an
unusual wall display.

CADENZA, Dinner Plate, $15.

SPRAY, Dinner Plate, $15.

WILLOW, Bread and Butter Plate, $5.

SKYLINE, TRAILWAYS, and PALISADES SHAPES

The earth tones of the times mark this somewhat less collectible era of pottery production. Competition from aggressive California Potteries and eventually from less expensive foreign producers prompted streamlined designs that are less popular with collectors. An advertisement in the July, 1954 issue *of Better Homes and Gardens* showed a typical homemaker announcing to other homemakers that one of the Skyline patterns pictures "was created just for you." An attempt to soften, and perhaps stimulate interest in a lagging market, resulted in the unique style of the Palisades line.

"SUNNY UP," Colonial, Dinner Plate, $15. SUNNY SPRAY, Salt Shaker, Pair $20. Teapot, $50.

SERENADE, Dinner Plate, $15.

SUNNY SPRAY, Ovide Coffee Pot $85. Creamer, $15. Blue Ridge advertised pattern as "CHEERFUL AS SUN-LIGHT."

FLOWER FANTASY, Dinner Plate, $15. Also called SPRAY RING.

DESERT FLOWER, Big Cup and Saucer, $45.

GREEN EYES, Cup and Saucer, $10. SERENITY, Plate, $10. DOE EYES is a variation of this pattern.

DESERT FLOWER, Cup and Saucer, $15.

CHEERIO (YELLOW), Covered Vegetable, $50.

"THRALL," Dinner Plate, $10.

CHEERIO (GREEN), 7" Square Plate, $20.

LUNA, Dinner Plate, $15. LUNA was often advertised as a Trailway pattern.

HALF PENNEY, Dinner Plate, $20.
Rope Handle accessories complement
this pattern.

PATRICIA, Dinner Plate, $15.

GOLD PATRICIA, Dinner Plate, $15.

GREENUP, Dinner Plate, $15.

GREENSVILLE, Dinner Plate, $15.
Sugar, $20. Creamer, $15.

(Left to right) KISMET, Saucer, $5. Two
sprays on full pattern. CECILLA, Saucer, $5. Blooming brown bud completes
this on full pattern.

CAROLINE, Cup and Saucer, $20. Also
found on Woodcrest shape.

PRELUDE, Dinner Plate, $15. Advertised by Sears in their Summer, 1954 catalogue.

BLOOMINGDALE, Dinner Plate, $10. It has been suggested that this pattern was designed for Bloomingdales Department Store.

BLOOMINGDALE, Palisades, Pitcher, $45.

FANTASIA Creamer, $15. Bread and Butter Plate, $5.

SARASOTA, Demi Sugar, $40. Dinner Plate, $15. Pepper Shaker, Pair $25.

TROPICAL, Dinner Plate, $15.

FAIRMONT, 7" Cereal Bowl, $10.

CALADIUM, Dinner Plate, $15.

BLOOMINGDALE, Ovide Coffeepot Lamp, $125.

FRENCH KNOTS, Cereal Bowl, $5. This pattern was also made by Stetson China Company.

"FATHER," Big Cup and Saucer, $35.

FRENCH KNOTS, Sugar Bowl, $25. Late Trailway style Sugar Bowl.

"TWIRLING TRIO," Dinner Plate, $20. The wide borders of TRAILWAY were not very popular when first introduced and are only moderately popular with today's collectors.

UPSTART, Cereal Bowl, $5.

MEDALLION, Dinner Plate, $20.

Backstamp for "TWIRLING TRIO," Pattern #4561-3, indicates that this pattern is a variation of a previously existing pattern.

Creamer. Made by Stetson China Company. MODERN LEAF, 14" Platter, $20. Made by Southern Potteries. Example of a pattern used by more than one china company.

YELLOW NOCTURNE, Barrel Shakers, Pair $25. Dinner Plate, $20.

MIDAS TOUCH, Dinner Plate, $20.

SOUTHERN DOGWOOD, Dinner Plate, $15.

ARTFUL, 7" Square Plate, $25.

GLORIOSA, Fruit Bowl, $5.

"FAYE," Cereal Bowl, $10.

VALDOSTA, Dinner Plate, $15.

RED RAMBLER, Snack Plate with cup, $35.

BONABELLA, 14" Platter, $30.

WRINKLED ROSE, Dinner Plate, $15. This was a reissue of a very popular Colonial pattern.

TEA ROSE, Dinner Plate, $20.

SUN BOUQUET, Salt Shaker, Pair, $20. This pattern was a repeat of a successful Colonial pattern.

Backstamp found on more delicate Skyline patterns, such as TEA ROSE and MARGARET ROSE.

MARGARET ROSE, Dinner Plate, $20.

UNAKA, Dinner Plate, $15. JENNY is a very similar patterns.

CHLOE, 14" Platter, $20.

WINNIE, Cup, $5. Bread and Butter Plate, $5.

TINY, Dinner Plate, $10.

"RED GAIETY," Saucer, $5.

DARCY, Dessert Plate, $15.

SABILLA, Cup and Saucer, $15.

MAYFLOWER, Cup, $5. Dinner Plate, $15.

TWIN FLOWERS, Fruit Bowl, $5.

BUCHANAN, Dinner Plate, $15.

"THORNY MAYFLOWER," Dinner Plate, $15.

"RED NOCTURNE," Dinner Plate, $25. Repeat of a popular Colonial pattern on Skyline shape.

JAPANESE WALLFLOWER, Divided Vegetable Bowl, $25.

MAYFLOWER BLUE, Dinner Plate, $20. Salt and Pepper Shakers, Pair $25.

PYRACANTHA, Cup and Saucer, $15.

BITTERSWEET, Salt Shaker, Pair $25. Dinner Plate, $15.

FOXFIRE, Cup, $10. Dinner Plate, $20.

NIGHT FLOWER, Soup Bowl, $20. Salt and Pepper Shakers, Pair $30. These shakers can be used with many patterns.

"BUTTERSCOTCH," Soup Bowl, $20. This line was introduced in 1952 as "color on color."

SUSAN, Butter Dish with lid, $35. Butter dish can also be used with SUSAN'S RING. "CARAMEL SUNDAE," Lace Edge, 9" Bowl, $25.

MOSS ROSE, Bread and Butter Plate, $10.

LABURNAN, Divided Vegetable Bowl, $25.

SUSAN, Dinner Plate, $15.

ATLANTA, Apple Shape Shakers, Pair $20.

FLOWER BARRELS, Dinner Plate, $25.

ATLANTA, Dinner Plate, $20.

SONATA, Gravy Stand, $20. 3" width is just wide enough to hold a gravy boat. It is sometimes called a Pickle Dish.

"LUCILLE," Dinner Plate, $15.

SONATA, Cereal Bowl, $10.

GILLEYFLOWER, Dinner Plate, $15.

115

"GLENNA," Cup and Saucer, $10.

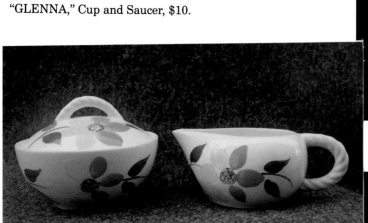

"GLENNA," Rope Handle Sugar and Creamer, Set, $40. This style accessory softened the Skyline and Woodcrest styles in an effort to adapt to the changing tastes of American homemakers.

ISOBEL, DINNER Plate, $10.

"GOLDEN STACCATO," Dinner Plate, $15. A lazy susan in this pattern has been found.

STACCATO, Palisades, Fruit Bowl, $5. COLUMBINE, Fruit Bowl, $5.

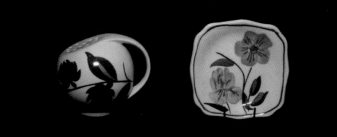

RED CLOVER, Pepper Shaker, Pair $25. GARDEN LANE, Ashtray, $20.

FOREST FRUIT, Creamer, $20. Dinner Plate, $20.

CLOVER, Dinner Plate, $20. Also found with pink Trailway border.

CROWNVETCH, Dinner Plate, $15.

LA VALETTE, Tab Bowl, $10.

FRENCH VIOLETS, Sugar $25. 13" Platter, $30.

VIOLET SPRAY, Gravy Boat, $20. Dinner Plate, $20.

"LOLLIE," Salt Shaker, Pair $25.

EVENING FLOWER, Teapot, $75. Sugar with lid, $20.

Glassware to match EVENING FLOWER.

NASSAU, Cup, $10. Advertised in 1942 Montgomery Ward catalogue.

CONFECTION, Saucer, $5.

PEGGY, Cereal Bowl, $5.

MOUNTAIN SWEETBRIAR, Cup and Saucer, $20.

PINKIE, 13" Platter, $15. Green edge distinguishes this pattern from PEGGY.

FLOWERET, Sugar with lid, $20. Full pattern has two flowers.

FLOWERET, Barrel Salt and Pepper Shakers, Pair $20.

CHESTON, Cup, $5. Full pattern has one red flower and two buds. Also found on Woodcrest shape.

PLANTATION IVY, Wall Lamp, $25.

Ashtray and glass to complement
PLANTATION IVY.

Back view of PLANTATION IVY Lamp
made with plate, cup, and saucer.

Stanley Home Products aluminum "get
acquainted" coaster, backstamp for
STANHOME IVY, coaster commemorat-
ing 45th anniversary of Stanley.

Frosted syrup jugs to match PLANTA-
TION IVY.

STANHOME IVY, 17" Platter, $40.

BALTIC IVY, Coffee carafe with stand, $60. Originally sold for $3.49.

KENILWORTH, Dinner Plate, $10.

ENGLISH IVY, Saucer, $5.

Stand for carafe.

BLACK MING, 17" Platter, $50. Also found on Woodcrest shape.

BALTIC IVY, Salt and Pepper Shakers, Pair $20. Dinner Plate, $10.

"WILD WILLOW," Dinner Plate, $20. ROBIN is another blue background Skyline pattern.

GRAY SMOKE, Dinner Plate, $15.

COWETA, Dinner Plate, $15. Spiegel Catalogue Pattern, 1948.

BONSAI, Dinner Plate, $25.

"HERB GARDEN," Dinner Plate, $20.

Backstamp on BONSAI reads "Westphall China Company."

SPRING WILLOW, Dinner Plate, $15.

CATTAILS, Dinner Plate, $20.

PUSSY WILLOW, 14" Platter, $25.

CATTAILS, Ovide Coffee Pot, $100.

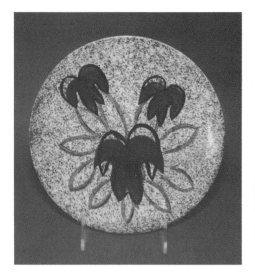

UGLEE, Dinner Plate, $15. Similar pattern in rust color called RAZZLE DAZZLE.

HOPS, Plate, $15. Also found in blue.

Linen towel with wheat embroidery.

"HARVEST OATS," Salad Plate, $20. Creamer, $20.

THISTLE, Cup and Saucer, $20.

WHEAT, Creamer, $20. Dinner Plate, $15. Blue Ridge advertised that pattern as GOLDEN WHEAT. A service for one, (five pieces) sold for 99c.

QUEEN ANNE'S LACE, Covered Sugar, $25. Dinner Plate, $20.

TRINKET, Dinner Plate, $15.

SPRIG, Cup, $5. This Trailway pattern was also produced with pink flowers on Skyline shape.

ROCKCASTLE, 8" Plate, $15.

SPRIG, Creamer, $15. This 50's shape was used with Trailway.

ROCK GARDEN, Dinner Plate, $15.

"CORONET," Fruit Bowl $5.

GOLDEN BELLS, Bread and Butter Plate, $5. Also found on Palisades shape.

"BONAIRE VARIANT," Dinner Plate, $15. The dark green leaves are not found on BONAIRE.

Backstamp with "Detergent Proof, Oven Safe" added to the Blue Ridge logo stamp, usually found on Skyline, Trailway, and Palisades patterns.

COSMOS, Rope Handle Creamer, $20. Rope Handle accessory pieces were often designed to complement more than one pattern.

Assortment of Skyline Shakers, Pair $40.

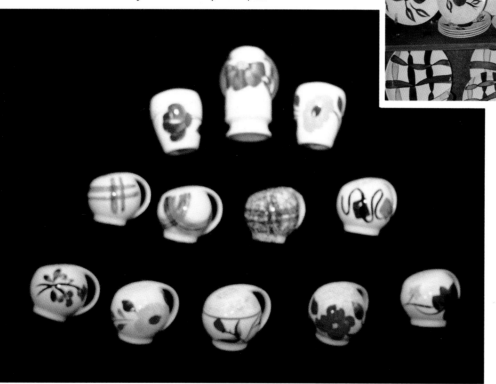

Blue Ridge display shelf in Georgia shop which specializes in Blue Ridge.

Palisades Shakers (Left to right) GRASSFLOWER (RUE-DE-LA-PAIZ0, PINK DOGWOOD, KIMBERLY, STAR SHOWER, PINK DOGWOOD.

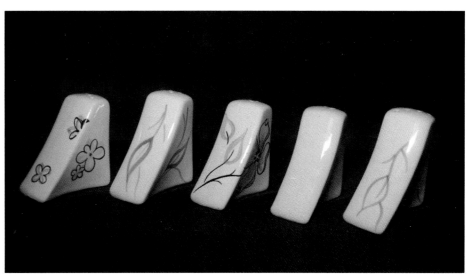

PINK DOGWOOD, Palisades, Teapot, $95. Dinner Plate, $25. Also called ROSEY.

Palisades Shakers, 2 3/8"x 2 1/4". The leaves are so similar on many of the Palisades patterns that these shakers are easily interchangeable.

WATER FLOWER, Snack Plate, $25 with Cup.

"WILLIAM'S LEAVES," 15" Platter, $25.

Multilevel stow'n show plate rack.

HOPEWELL, Dinner Plate, $15.

"BLUEFIELD VARIANT," Creamer, $15. Same name for a different pattern. See index.

125

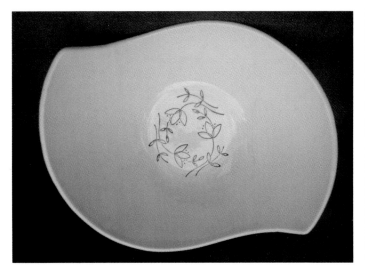

LAUREL BLOOMERY, 9" Bowl, $25.

"SWEET GUM," Sugar and Creamer Set, $40.

(Left to right) HARVESTTIME, Fruit Bowl, $5. Also called HOPS WITH BOW. TRIANGLE, Saucer, $5.

CHIFFON, 15" Platter, $25. Pattern also found without gray edge.

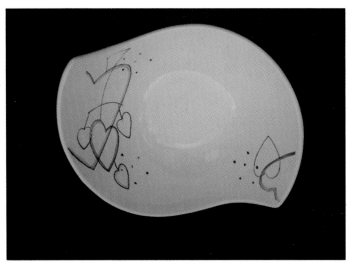

HEART THROB, 9" Bowl, $25.

BLUE RIDGE is a name often seen on products in the Blue Ridge Mountains.

WOODCREST SHAPE

Despite a Blue Ridge advertisement in a 1953 *Better Homes and Gardens* magazine depicting "modern-minded homemakers loud in praise of Woodcrest charm," this shape was not particularly popular with homemakers of the fifties. The painters appropriately dubbed it "burlap" because the textured surface was created by lining the molds with burlap. Several Skyline patterns were adapted to and reproduced on the textured shape, hence the similarity of SUNRISE and COCK-O-THE-MORN. Woodcrest is easier to identify than to find because it was not successful enough to be produced in great quantities. Because of its limited production, unusual texture, and uniquely shaped accessory pieces, it is eagerly sought after by many collectors of 1950s china.

AQUA LEAF, Dinner Plate, $25.

"JACOB'S LEAVES," Dinner Plate, $25.

MING TREE, Saucer, $10.

"PUSSY TOES," Soup Bowl, $15.

APRIL, Dinner Plate, $25. Advertised in House Beautiful in 1954.

"SCARLETT," Dinner Plate, $30.

PATCHWORK, Tab Bowl, $20.

ABINGDON, Tab Bowl, $15.

BAMBOO, Cup and Saucer, $25. Note the square bottom. Advertised in Montgomery Ward catalogue as BAL HAI.

TEASEL, Dinner Plate, $30.

BLACK BOTTOM, Dinner Plate, $25.

ECHO, One section of a lazy susan, $20.

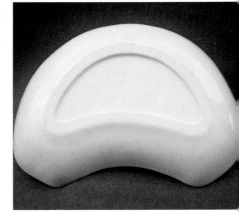

Bottom of ECHO dish shaped to fit into wooden tray.

Backstamp found on most Woodcrest patterns.

The textile industry capitalized on popularity of 50's Woodcrest patterns with a variety of coordinating cotton tablecloths.

QUILTED IVY, Gravy Boat, $45.

Chapter 4
Fruit and Vegetable Patterns

Mouthwatering fruit, artistically placed on a variety of shapes, has whet the appetite of many Blue Ridge collectors. Finding their way into the homes of America today, once more, they decorate kitchens and family rooms. Several fruit sets, complete with an assortment of accessories were advertised in magazines and sold through catalogues in the 1940s and 1950s, therefore availability is not a problem even when assembling sets for actual use.

FRUIT PUNCH, Platter, $1,200. One of a kind, signed by painters of Crew 92, August 3, 1944.

Reverse of artists' signed platter, inscribed: "Memory of the S.P.I., Dora Poore."

"CARL'S FRUIT BOWL," Lotus Leaf, 9"
bowl, $25.

FLOWERING BERRY, Candlewick,
Dinner Plate, $20.

MARY, Astor, Tab Bowl, $20.

·"CLINCHFIELD FRUIT," Clinchfield,
Dinner Plate, $25.

FLOWERING BERRY, Candlewick,
Cup, $10.

GRAPE WINE, Snub Nose Teapot,
$125.

MARY, Astor, 13" Platter, $25.

"LEAFY FRUIT RING," Astor, 15" Platter, $30.

SPRING FEVER, Clinchfield, 12" Platter, $30.

(Left) "SEA MIST, " Helen Pitcher, $145.
(Right) GRAPES, Helen Pitcher, $125.

FREEDOM RING, Astor, Dinner Plate, $30.

VINEYARD, Astor, Dinner Plate, $25.

GRAPE HARVEST, Colonial, Dinner Plate, $25.

DELLA ROBBIA, Piecrust, Dinner Plate, $30.

WINERY, Clinchfield, Dinner Plate, $25.

CHABLIS, Colonial, Dinner Plate, $15.

GRAPE SALAD, Candlewick, 10" Salad Serving Bowl, $50. Salad Servers (fork and spoon) were also made.

LEMONADE, Colonial, Vegetable Bowl, $25.

GOOSEBERY, Candlewick, Saucer $5.

"HEARD IT ON THE VINE," 6" Square Plate, $30.

SCUPPERNOG, Astor, Demi Teapot, $125. Covered Toast, $120.

BETHANY BERRY, Skyline, Fruit Bowl, $5.

(Left) STILL LIFE, Colonial, Cake Plate, $40. (Right) Dinner Plate, $25. (Front) Cup and Saucer, $20.

"AUTUMN STILL LIFE," Colonial, Cake Plate, $45.

TUTTI-FRUITI, Colonial, Big Cup and
Saucer, $50.

TUTTI-FRUITI, Colonial, Dinner Plate,
$30.

FAIRMEDE FRUITS, Astor, Dinner
Plate, $25. Egg Cup, $35.

WILD STRAWBERRY, Colonial, Collection of Sue and Jeff Beaulieu.

STILL LIFE, Colonial, Cup and Saucer,
$20.

BERRYVILLE, Colonial, 13" Platter,
$25.

MOUNTAIN STRAWBERRY, Skyline, Dinner Plate, $20.

STRAWBERRY RING, Trailway, Soup Bowl, $10.

FRAGERIA, Skyline, Luncheon Plate, $15.

STRAWBERRY SUNDAE, Colonial, Cereal Bowl, $10.

CHERRY DROPS, Colonial, Dinner Plate, $25.

Cherry Bounce, Colonial, Dinner Plate, $20. Pattern number we were given for this pattern indicates that it was designed to be a variation of CRAB APPLE.

"STRAWBERRY LUSTRE," Lace Edge, Fruit Set: 9" Bowl and six Fruit Bowls, $60.

Frosted 8 ounce glasses to match various patterns. Made by several glass companies.

"AQUA WILD CHERRY" (#4) Skyline, Saucer, $5. SPIDER-WEB (Black), Skyline, Cup, $5.

Attractive table setting combining "AQUA WILD CHERRY" (#4), Skyline dinnerware and SPIDERWEB (Black), Skyline accessory pieces.

"PINK WILD CHERRY" (#2) Skyline, 7" Square Plate, $25.

CHERRY WINE, Piecrust, 14" Platter, $40.

CHERRY WINE, Piecrust, Sugar, $25, Creamer, $20.

CHERRYWOOD, Skyline, Cup, $5.

"EARTHY WILD CHERRY" (#3) Piecrust, Creamer, $15, Dinner Plate, $20. "SIMPLY WILD CHERRY" (#1) Skyline completes the WILD CHERRY patterns.

DOUBLE CHERRY, Skyline, Rope Handle Gravy Boat, $25.

CHERRY COKE, Colonial, 14" Platter, $30.

QUARTET, Candlewick, 12" Platter, $20.

MOUNTAIN CHERRIES, Skyline, 13" Platter, $20. Also known as HERMITAGE.

"CHERRY, CHERRY," Candlewick, Dinner Plate, $20. This pattern is similar to NORTH STAR CHERRY.

CHERRY TREE GLEN, Piecrust, Bread and Butter Plate, $10. Also called CHERRY CLUSTERS.

MOUNTAIN CHERRY, Candlewick, Dinner Plate, $20.

DELICIOUS, Candlewick, 13" Platter, $25.

MOUNTAIN CRAB, Colonial, Saucer, $5. Sugar, $25.

MOUNTAIN CRAB, Leftover Container, $40.

Backstamp on Leftover: " Mountain Crab, Blue Ridge Mountains, Hand Art,"

DELICIOUS, Ball Teapot, $125.

Quaker Oats boxes with premium offer. Quaker Oats literally put apples on American tables.

"TWIN APPLES," Candlewick, Vegetable Bowl, $25.

Quaker shipping box containing Cup, Saucer, Fruit Bowl, and Bread and Butter Plate, $100.

QUAKER APPLE, Candlewick, Dinner Plate, $20. Pottery photographs show this pattern was also marketed as "OLD ORCHARD."

"NEW APPLE," Salt and Pepper Shakers, 2 1/4", Pair $40.

Quaker Oats box with Spoon Rest premium offer.

QUAKER APPLE, Candlewick, Original shipping box opened to show cup. Cup, $10.

APPLE, Salt and Pepper Shakers, Pair $25. Quaker Oats offered these at a cost of 25 cents.

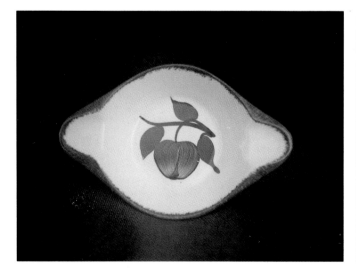

BIG APPLE, Spoon Rest, $40. The cost of this item was 40 cents plus the blue star from the Quaker box.

APPLE CRISP, Skyline, Saucer, $5. BIG APPLE, Colonial, Cup, $5.

BIG APPLE, Colonial, Dinner Plate, $25.

CRISS CROSS, Piecrust, Luncheon Plate, $20.

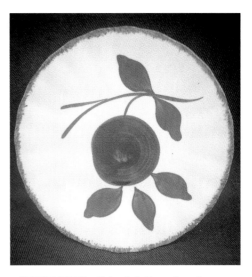

APPLE TRIO, Colonial, Bread and Butter Plate, $5.

PIPPIN, Skyline, Bread and Butter, $5. Also called Valencia.

"TEACHER'S PET," Colonial, Salad Plate, $25.

APPLE TRIO, Colonial, Dinner Plate, $20.

BIG APPLE, Egg Cup, $40.

APPLE CRUNCH, Piecrust, 12" Platter, $25.

APPLE TWIG, Colonial, Tab Bowl, $25.

SWEETIE PIE, Colonial, Square Plate, $25. Saucer, $5.

RED APPLE, Colonial, Divided Warming Dish, $45.

APPLE TART, Colonial, Dinner Plate, $20.

APPLE CRISP, Skyline, Bread and Butter Plate, $10.

FRUIT FANTASY, Ashtray, $20. RED APPLE, China Shaker, Pair $85.

GRANNY SMITH APPLE, Skyline, Soup Bowl, $15.

FANTASY APPLE, Skyline, Dinner Plate, $20.

BEADED APPLE, Colonial, Creamer and Sugar, (Set) $45.

JUNE APPLE, Woodcrest, Soup Bowl, $20.

BEADED APPLE, Colonial, Cup and Saucer, $20. BEADED CHERRY is a very similar pattern.

JUNE APPLE, Woodcrest, Teapot, $150.

ARLINGTON APPLE, Palisades, Tab Bowl, $20.

AUTUMN APPLE, Dinner Plate, $25. Blue Ridge advertisements describe this pattern as symbolizing "the bounty of nature."

ARLINGTON APPLE, Skyline, 12" Platter, $20.

WINESAP, Skyline, Cup, $10. CRAB APPLE, Colonial, Cup, $10. Most CRAB APPLE collectors prefer the cup with two apples.

APPLE JACK, Skyline, Salt and Pepper Shakers, Pair $25. Egg Cup, $30.

"SKY APPLES," Skyline, Salt and Pepper Shakers, Pair $25. Collectors of several apple patterns claim these as belonging to their pattern, so we decided to simply call them "SKY APPLES".

APPLE JACK, Skyline, Dinner Plate, $25. Cup, $10.

CRAB APPLE, Boot Vase, $95.

CRAB APPLE, Colonial, Display Shelf with 7" Square Plate, $25. Fruit Bowl, $5. Tab Bowl, $20. Cup, $10. Juice glass.

APPLE JACK, Wall Lamp, $30.

APPLING, Colonial, Vegetable Bowl,
$30.

GRAY APPLE, Skyline, Dinner Plate,
$25.

FRUIT BASKET, Chocolate Pot, $225.

MOD APPLE, Skyline, Snack Plate,
$25.

FRUIT BASKET, Leaf Celery, $65.
Maple Leaf Relish, $80.

CANDIED FRUIT, Leaf Relish, $60.

CANDIED FRUIT, Sally Pitcher, $175.

ANJOU, Skyline, Cup and Saucer, $20.

FAYETTE FRUIT, Candlewick, Dinner Plate, $25.

BARTLETT, Candlewick, Dinner Plate, $20.

PORTIA'S PEARS, Palisades, Dessert Plate, $20. Also found on Skyline.

APPLE & PEAR, 7" Square Plate, $25. Found on Skyline and Woodcrest.

RIDGE HARVEST, Piecrust, Vegetable Bowl, $20.

BOUNTEOUS, Piecrust, Snack Plate, $20. Very similar pattern on Candlewick is called FRUIT MEDLEY.

TWIN PEAR, Candlewick, Vegetable Bowl, $25.

SWEET AND SOUR, Colonial, Dinner Plate, $25.

FARLEY'S FRUIT, Skyline, Bread and Butter, $10.

FRUIT SHERBET, Colonial, Creamer, $20. Dinner Plate, $25.

FRUIT PUNCH, Colonial, Dinner Plate, $20. Cup $5.

FRUIT PUNCH, Colonial, Teapot, $100. Note: Lid is for Piecrust teapot.

FRUIT PUNCH, 4 1/2" Spiral Pitcher, $110.

FRUIT FANTASY, Milady Pitcher, $200.

FRUIT STAND, Colonial, Bread and Butter Plate, $10.

FRUIT SALAD, Colonial, Dinner Plate, $15.

FRUIT FANTASY, Deep Shell, $65.

"FONDEVILLE PUNCH," Colonial, Desert Plate, $10. One of several fruit patterns made for and stamped "FONDEVILLLE, NEW YORK."

FRUIT FANTASY, Colonial, Open Sugar, $25. Snack Plate, $30. China Shaker, Pair $75. Cup, $10.

FRUIT FANTASY, Colonial, China Shakers, Pair $75.

BOUNTIFUL, Colonial, Dinner Plate, $25.

Country hutch with sculptured fruit pitchers and Hall's McCormick teapots, which blend very well with many Blue Ridge patterns.

FRUIT FANTASY, Small Ramekin, $35.

SCULPTURED FRUIT, Pitchers, 7 1/2", $85. 7", $95. 6 1/2", $85.

ORCHARD GLORY, Colonial, Dinner Plate, $20.

Backstamp of 7 1/2" SCULPTURED FRUIT PITCHER. This size was referred to as "deluxe" in advertising literature.

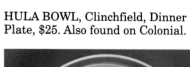

HULA BOWL, Clinchfield, Dinner Plate, $25. Also found on Colonial.

HAWAIIAN FRUIT, Candlewick, Dinner Plate, $25.

DIXIE HARVEST, Piecrust, Luncheon Plate, $20.

QUILTED FRUIT, Skyline, Creamer, $20.

HAWAIIAN FRUIT, Trailway, Cup and Saucer, $25. Also found on Astor.

FOLK ART FRUIT, Ovide Coffee Pot, $125.

QUILTED FRUIT, Woodcrest, Dinner Plate, $30.

HAWAIIAN FRUIT, Piecrust, Dinner Plate, $20.

QUILTED FRUIT, Skyline, Rope Handle Creamer and Sugar, Set $55. Salad Plate, $20.

COUNTRY FRUIT, Trailway, Bread and Butter Plate, $10. Full pattern has matching yellow apple. Shown in Ward's catalogues, with matching glassware, as CALICO.

"QUILTED STRAWBERRY," Woodcrest, 7" Square Plate, $30. QUILTED FRUIT, Woodcrest, Salt and Pepper Shakers, Pair $45.

TIC TACK, Piecrust, 14" Platter, $40. Custard Cup, $25.

GINGHAM APPLE, Skyline, Cup and Saucer, $20.

GINGHAM FRUIT, Skyline, Butter Dish, $45.

SHADOW FRUIT, Palisades, Pitcher, $45. SHADOW FRUIT, Skyline, Dinner Plate, $20. Note pink border on Skyline plate.

GINGHAM FRUIT, Trailway, Dinner Plate, $25.

CALICO FARM, Skyline, Handled Snack Plate, $30.

SHADOW FRUIT, Trailway, Cup, $10. Bread and Butter Plate, $10.

FRUIT COCKTAIL (APPLES), Astor, Salad Plate, $25.

FRUIT COCKTAIL (GRAPES), Astor, Salad Plate, $25.

HONOLULU (TWO PEARS), Candlewick, Salad Plate, $25.

FRUIT COCKTAIL (PEARS), Astor, Salad Plate, $25.

FRUIT COCKTAIL (POMEGRAN-ATES), Astor, Salad Plate, $25.

HONOLULU (THREE FIGS), Candlewick, Salad Plate, $25.

FRUIT COCKTAIL (PLUMS), Astor, Salad Plate, $25.

FRUIT COCKTAIL (FIGS), Astor, Salad Plate, $25.

HONOLULU (TWO APPLES), Candlewick, Salad Plate, $25.

HONOLULU (THREE APPLES),
Candlewick, Salad Plate, $25.

"JUBILEE PLUMS," Colonial, Salad
Plate, $25.

"JUBILEE PEARS," Colonial, 10" Salad
Serving Bowl, $40.

HONOLULU (CHERRIES),
Candlewick, Salad Plate, $25.

"JUBILEE CHERRIES," Colonial,
Salad Plate, $25.

HONOLULU (WHITE GRAPES),
Candlewick, Salad Plate, $25.

JUBILEE FRUIT SET (VINTAGE), Colonial, 12" Platter,
$30. The platter for the Jubilee Fruit Set contains many of
the fruit, which are seen on the individual salad plates.

STRAWBERRY PATCH, Colonial, Salad Plate, $25.

COUNTY FAIR (POMEGRANATE AND GRAPES), Candlewick, Salad Plate, $25.

(Left to right) GRAPES and PEACH AND STRAWBERRIES.

COUNTY FAIR, Colonial, Cup and Saucer, $25. Because Avon rewarded dealers and cultivated customers with these plates, they are generally referred to as the Avon Fruit Set. However, the set was also marketed by several retail and mail order companies. Advertised as "Hand Painted Beauties" by a Springfield company and as the "Pick of the Crop" by a Pittsburgh company; a set of eight plates could be purchased for only $4.95 Postpaid. At this price "Anyone would love a set" advertised a New York company.

JUBILEE, Colonial, Creamer, $20. Sugar (Lid only), $5.

"JUBILEE POMEGRANATE," Colonial, Salad Plate, $25.

COUNTY FAIR (GRAPES), Colonial, Salad Plate, $25.

COUNTY FAIR (PEACH AND STRAWBERRIES), Colonial, Salad Plate, $25.

COUNTY FAIR (PEARS), Colonial, Salad Plate, $25.

COUNTY FAIR (POMEGRANATE AND GRAPES), Colonial, Salad Plate, $25.

COUNTY FAIR (CHERRIES), Colonial, Salad Plate, $25.

(Left to right) PEAR and PEACH.

(Left to right) GRAPES AND POME-GRANATE and PEAR AND CHERRIES

(Left to right) CHERRIES and PLUMS.

COUNTY FAIR (PEACHES), Colonial, Salad Plate, $25.

COUNTY FAIR (PLUMS), Colonial, Salad Plate, $25.

COUNTY FAIR (PEAR AND CHER-RIES), Colonial, Salad Plate, $25.

COUNTY FAIR, Candlewick, Salad Serving Bowl, 10 1/4", $40. This salad set is not often found on Candlewick.

DUFF SALAD SET (PLUMS), Candlewick, Salad Plate, $25.

DUFF SALAD SET (PEACH AND STRAWBERRIES), Candlewick, Salad Plate, $25.

DUFF SALAD SET (GRAPES), Candlewick, Salad Plate, $25.

DUFF SALAD SET (PEAR), Candlewick, Salad Plate, $20.

DUFF SALAD SET (POMEGRANATE AND GRAPES), Candlewick, Salad Plate, $25.

DUFF SALAD SET(ORANGE), Candlewick, Salad Plate, $25.

KING'S
HAND PAINTED
UNDERGLAZE
MADE IN U.S.A.

Back stamp for King's, one of many companies who purchased this fruit set from Southern. This accounts for the variety of swirled backgrounds found. The set was also advertised as "Gay Airs", plates for decorative or culinary use. A set of eight plates, offered in a variety of sizes, sold for $5.50, postpaid.

DUFF SALAD SET (PEAR AND CHER-RIES), Candlewick, Salad Plate, $25.

DUFF SALAD SET (CHERRIES), Candlewick, Salad Plate, $25.

VEGGIE (CARROT AND SCALLIONS), Skyline, Snack Plate, $30. Others in this set are: tomatoes, turnip, and peas. Also found on lazy Susan.

Handmade Bib.

Country hutch with assorted fruit patterns.

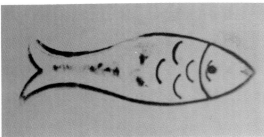

Stamp for TUNA SALAD pattern. This Skyline pattern featured two large and two small fish on a dinner plate.

VEGETABLE SOUP, Skyline, Salad Serving Bowl, $40. Has "Vitamin Frolics" back stamp.

Chapter 5
A Potpourrie of Patterns

Blue Ridge Barn storage buildings.

MING TREE dinner plate on door of Blue Ridge Barn.

Many Blue Ridge collectors, at one time or another, travel to Tennessee to shop at the Blue Ridge Barn and visit with Ray and Mary Farley. After they recover from the shock of so much Blue Ridge in one place, they might be lucky enough to eat a

delicious meal out of Mary's tab soup bowls in, of course, the MARY pattern. Don't forget to see the famous toothed parrot plate tucked in with other rarities.

Inside the Blue Ridge Barn shelves are filled with numerous patterns of Blue Ridge dinnerware, which have been identified, inventoried, priced and are ready for eager buyers from all over the United States.

Five-digit number near Blue Ridge backstamp is part of the Farley's well-organized inventory system. Numbers are easily washed off.

RICHMOND, Trellis, Bread and Butter Plate, $25.

RICHMOND backstamp.

"RINGED LEAF," Lace Edge Pitcher, $90. This is a very unusual pitcher.

FLAME, Dinner Plate, $10.

"FLATLINE," Clinchfield, Dinner Plate, $25.

LEAF, Astor, Dinner Plate, $15.

"VICTORIAN," Martha Pitcher, $95. Stamped "#2 Martha Jug Dec.#1."

BEDECKED, Skyline, Cup and Saucer, $10. Dinner Plate, $15.

"BLUE LEAF," Colonial, Dinner Plate, $20.

"PASTEL LEAF," Cake Plate, $40. Cake Lifter, $20. Lifters are 9" in length and measure 3" in width.

LEAF, Cake Plate, $40.

RED LEAF, Clinchfield, 7 1/4" x 5 1/4" x 3 1/4", Gravy Plate, $15. ANTIQUE LEAF, Lacy Scroll Edge, Creamer, $30.

"PINK PLUMES," Martha, Set of 5 mixing bowls, $150.

"RUSSELLVILLE VARIANT," Candlewick, Dinner Plate, $20.

RUSSELLVILLE, Candlewick, Dinner Plate, $20.

LOUISIANA LACE, Candlewick, Dinner Plate, $15.

"BLUE ICE," Candlewick, 9" Bowl, $30. Also found in green. Martha Pitcher, $60.

MARTHA, Pitchers, $50 each. These pitchers were made in a variety of colors and 6 1/4" and 5 3/4" sizes. They are seldom marked.

LACE & LINES, Candlewick, Dinner Plate, $10.

"PINK LACE," Candlewick, Dinner Plate, $15.

BARBERRY, Candlewick, Dinner Plate, $!5.

"PARK PLACE," Candlewick, Dinner Plate, $20.

"LOUISIANA HEARTS," Candlewick, (Red Line) Bread and Butter Plate, $5 each. (Blue Line) Fruit Bowl, $5.

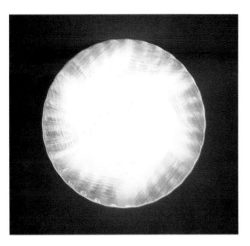

"RED BUZZ STAR," Colonial, Dinner Plate, $10. BUZZ STAR, Colonial is blue.

"X'S & O'S," Scroll Edge, 9" Bowl, $25.

JUNGLE GRASS (BLACK), Woodcrest, Teapot, $100.

"MODERN TOAST," Woodcrest, Dinner Plate, $20.

JUNGLE GRASS (BLACK), Skyline, Teapot, $60. Ovide, Coffee Pot with lid, $90. Salt and Pepper Set, $30.

SQUARES, Skyline, Salt Shaker, Pair $25. Dinner Plate, $20.

"SIGNALS," Skyline, Dinner Plate, $15. Similar pattern with red flags found on Piecrust shape.

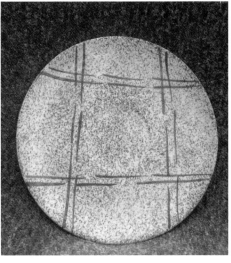

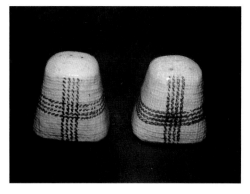

SCATTER PLAID, Skyline, Gravy Boat, $10. Also appropriately called HIT & MISS STENCIL.

JOHN'S PLAID, Skyline, Saucer, $3. Darker pattern called LORETTA.

STENCIL, Woodcrest, Salt and Pepper Shakers, Pair $35.

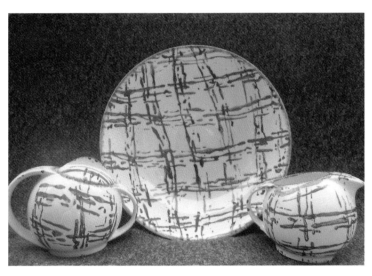

SCATTER PLAID, Skyline, Sugar with lid, $15. Creamer, $10. Soup Bowl, $10. Slight variation in plaid indicates different production dates.

"BARLEY PLAID," Skyline, Sugar with lid, $15. Teapot, $50.

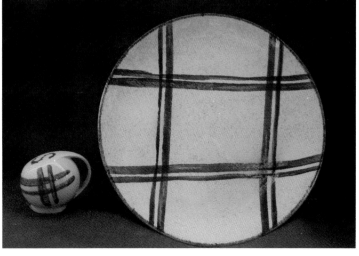

"WAVY PLAID," Skyline, Salt and Pepper Shakers, Pair $20. 12" Platter, $10.

BREAKFAST BAR, Skyline, Salt Shaker, Pair $20. Dinner Plate, $10.

BREAKFAST BAR, Ovide Coffee Pot, $70.

"ROUNDELAY," Trailway, Dinner Plate, $15. Bread and Butter Plate, $5. Blue Ridge advertised this pattern, which was made in yellow, pink, blue, and gray.

RUSTIC PLAID, Skyline, Sugar with lid, $15. Creamer, $10. Dinner Plate, $10.

"GREEN PLAID," Skyline, Salt Shaker, Pair $20. Dinner Plate, $10.

MAROON PLAID, Skyline, Creamer, $10. "BLUE PLAID," Skyline, Saucer, $3.

SILHOUETTE (BLACK) Skyline, Two-Tier Tidbit Server, $25. Palisades, 5" Square Plate, $15.

ORANGE SHERBET, Skyline, Cup and Saucer, $15.

SPIDERWEB (PINK), Palisades, 8" Square Plate, $15.

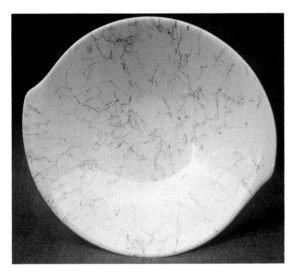

SPIDERWEB (BLUE), Palisades, Tab Bowl, $15.

SPIDERWEB (GREEN), Piecrust, Cup, $5. Skyline, Snack Plate, $10. Cups have white or color interiors.

SILHOUETTE (RED) Skyline, Bread and Butter Plate, $3.

"SO BLUE," Palisades, Pitcher, $45. "SO BLUE" Pitcher is compatible with almost every Palisades pattern. Unfinished Bisque Pitcher. It is interesting to note that because bisque is porous it must be fired once before applying a decal or paint. We seldom see Blue Ridge in this stage of its production.

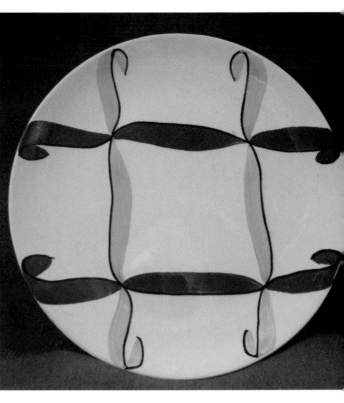

STREAMERS, Skyline, Dinner Plate, $10. This pattern was recognized by one pottery painter as an extremely difficult one to paint. To create the twisted ribbons of this seemingly simple pattern, it was necessary to literally twist a square paintbrush without lifting it from the surface while maintaining an even flow of paint.

RIBBON PLAID, Skyline, Dinner Plate, $10.

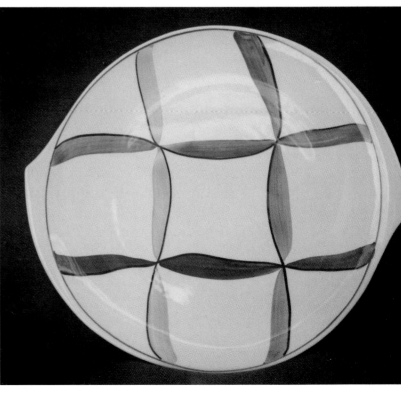

FESTIVE, Skyline, Dessert Plate, $5.

"TWISTED RIBBONS," Palisades, 12" Platter, $25.

Chapter 6
Special Patterns

TALISMAN WALLPAPER

Talisman Wallpaper Advertising Plate, $300. An advertisement in an October, 1953 *House Beautiful* magazine, announced that homemakers who were "a stickler for perfectionist matching" could now purchase coordinated wallpaper and dinnerware. What seemed like a novel idea was not wholeheartedly accepted in a world perhaps not quite ready for this concept. Today, collectors find it a challenge to hunt for these Blue Ridge-Talisman patterns. Since fewer rolls of wallpaper have survived than dinnerware, wallpaper is more of a challenge to find.

WOODBINE, Skyline, Dinner Plate, $25.

Backstamp for Talisman plates. TALISMAN WILD STRAWBERRY, similar to WILD STRAWBERRY, is also a Talisman pattern.

BLOSSOM TREE, Skyline, Bread and Butter Plate, $10. Sugar with lid, $25.

CHERRY TIME, Astor, Bread and Butter Plate, $10. Dinner Plate, $30.

YORKTIME, Colonial, Dinner Plate, $50.

DESIGNER SERIES

"FEATHERS," Clinchfield, $95.　　ABRACADABRA, Clinchfield, $95.

KALEIDOSCOPE, Clinchfield, $70.

"MAGGIE," Big Cup and Saucer, $45. The Designer Series, reportedly a limited production line, is quite unique in style. Originally thought to be only a salad set, collectors are finding other pieces of dinnerware such as this big cup and saucer belonging to Linda Smith.

NAUTICAL LINE

Bob and Wanda Woods with two of their favorite pieces, MARINER tea tile and MILLIE'S PRIDE spoon rest.

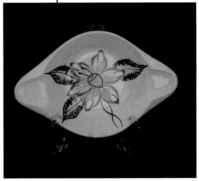

MILLIE'S PRIDE, Spoon Rest, $30.

Nautical Patterns (top to bottom) "CRUISING," Astor, Dinner Plate, $60. SAILBOAT, Astor, Bread and Butter Plate, $40.

MARINER, Tea Tile, $50.

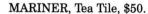

MARINER, Fruit Bowl, $20. Dinnerware has been found on Astor and Candlewick. Sea gulls seem to have flown away!!

SUNSET SAILS, Square Box, $120. Ash Tray, $20.

FEATHERED FRIENDS

Coordinating mallard tapestry.

PEACOCK, Candy Box, $250.

MALLARD, Salt and Pepper Shakers, $300 pair.

MALLARD DUCK Box, $600. Sometimes called STREAMSIDE. Rectangular ashtrays are painted with greenery only.

DREAMBIRDS, Colonial, Dinner Plate, $85.

NESTING BIRDS, (Left to right) Skyline, Fruit Bowl, $15. Trailway Fruit Bowl, $20.

Madelyn Kimmel-Holley shows round wood-framed bird plates from her collection. (Left to right) IVORY BILLED WOODPECKER, Skyline: WINTER WREN, Astor.

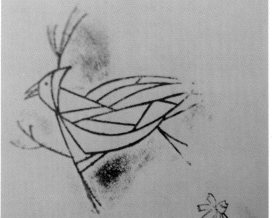

Southern Potteries' stamp for an unidentified bird. Perhaps this was an additional pattern designed to depict life in the branches. Southern artists depicted nature, especially the birds of Audubon and Gould, in their own style. Three salad sets were part of regular production.

SONGBIRDS (IVORY BILLED WOOD-PECKER,) Skyline, Luncheon Plate, $45.

SONGBIRDS (YELLOW SHAFTED FLICKER,) Skyline, Luncheon Plate, $45.

SONGBIRDS (SUMMER TANAGER,) Skyline, Luncheon Plate, $45.

SONGBIRDS (HOODED WARBLER,) Skyline, Luncheon Plate, $45. One-Tier Tidbit, $60. Not pictured: HUMMING-BIRD, CATBIRD, ORCHARD ORIOLE AND SCRUB JAY.

"WINTER WREN" SONG-
BIRDS, Astor, Salad Plate,
$45.

"LOGGERHEAD SHRIKE" SONG-
BIRDS, Astor, Salad Plate, $45.

"CARBONATED WARBLER" SONG-
BIRDS, Astor, Salad Plate, $45.

TUFTED TITMOUSE, Colonial, Dinner
Plate, $50.

OLD CROW, Colonial, Dinner Plate,
$50.

FORKTAILED FLYCATCHER, Colonial, Dinner Plate, $50.

GRAY KINGBIRD, Colonial, Dinner
Plate, $50.

WESTERN BLUEBIRD, Colonial, Dinner Plate, $50.

QUAIL, Colonial, 12" Plate, $800. Signed Frances Kyker. Slight differences will be found in plates by other artist signatures. Surprisingly, a set of these plates has reportedly been found, not by a collector..

QUAIL, Colonial, 12" Plate, $800. Signed Louise Guinn.

GREEN MILL, Clinchfield, 10" Plate, $650. Signed Ruby S. Hart Others in this series are WHITE MILL and GOLD CABIN.

Shelf with rare Character Jugs. Left to right are Paul
Revere, (6 1/4") $700, Pioneer Woman, (6 1/2") $700,
Indian, (6 3/4") $900 and Daniel Boone, (6") $700. Names
are incised on bases except for the INDIAN.

Virginia and Lincoln Barber with Character Jugs, their
favorite Blue Ridge pieces.

"MINIATURE PIONEER WOMAN," 4" Jug. Reportedly,
Macy's requested the pottery to make this petite Pioneer
Woman. Contrary to Macy's intent it proved to be too
expensive to make, resulting in only four being produced.

An unusual sight at an auction in Springfield, Missouri:
Three Pioneer Women and lots of Betsy Jugs.

PV (Peasant Village) backstamp on HAM 'n EGGS pattern. PV was the logo for Peasant village, a jobber that purchased from Southern and other potteries.

HAM 'n EGGS, Candlewick, Cup and Saucer, $50. Dessert Plate, $45.

BREEZY WINDOW, Candlewick, Bread and Butter Plate, $40.

COUNTRYSIDE backstamp. Patterns in this series not shown include: GARDEN FENCE and PEAS 'n POD.

EGG BASKET, Candlewick, Fruit Bowl, $30.

BLACKBERRY VINE, Candlewick, Dinner Plate, $80.

COCK-A-DOODLE, Skyline, Dinner Plate, $80.

COCK-A-DOODLE, Skyline, Cup and Saucer, $40.

"COLORFUL," Rooster and Hen Shakers, $125 pair.

"LITTLE GREEN APPLES," Skyline, Divided Vegetable, $45. Shakers, $50 pair.

Stamp with pattern for ROOSTER egg plate.

ROOSTER, Egg Plate, $125. Variations in roosters are common on this shape. Also, flowers are found on egg plates.

HIGH STEPPER, 6" Square Plate, $50. Also called COME AND GET IT.

ROOSTER, Candlewick, Motto Fruit Bowl, $30. Note "feet!"

SINGING ROOSTER, Square Plate, $70.

ROOSTER, Candlewick, Motto Plate, $95. Note "feet!"

JIGSAW, Skyline, Cereal Bowl, $40.
This particular piece is unpainted.

"DOMINICKERS," Salt and Pepper
Shakers, $125 pair.

GAME COCK, Clinchfield, Bread and
Butter Plate, $65.

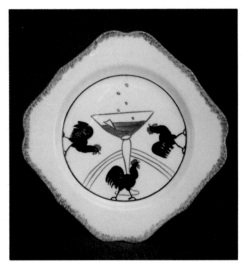

CHEERS, 6" Square Plate, $60.

COCKY-LOCKY, Clinchfield, Jumbo
Cup and Saucer, $75.

COCKY-LOCKY, Clinchfield, Soup
Bowl, $95.

Linen Placemat.

ROOSTER, Square Box, $125. Ash Tray,
$25.

174

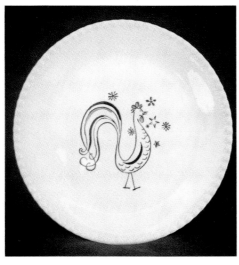

ROCKPORT ROOSTER, Candlewick, Dinner Plate, $50. Very similar pattern on Skyline called SLIM PICKINS.

"SILO," Skyline, Egg Cup, $60. From STREET'S BARNYARD pattern.

ROCKPORT ROOSTER, Skyline, Butter Dish with lid, $85.

"EARTHY," Earthenware Chick Pitcher, $75. Also in yellow.

WISHING WELL, Skyline, Cup and Saucer, $50.

"FLORA," China Chick Pitcher, $125.

WISHING WELL, Skyline, Dinner Plate, $50.

BLUE LINE FARM, Scroll Edge, 9" Bowl, $50.

"NEW LIFE," Chick Pitcher, $175.

CHANTICLEER, Skyline, Teapot, $125. Creamer, $45.

SUNRISE, Woodcrest, Dinner Plate, $60. Repetitive themes such as the rising sun, the distant barn and the crowing rooster on the fence, are found on SUNRISE, EVENTIDE AND COCK-O-THE-MORN.

CHICKEN PICKINS, Skyline, 15" Platter, $75.

COCK O' THE WALK, Candlewick, Dinner Plate, $45.

"WHITECASTLE," Salt and Pepper Shakers, $125 pair.

RED ROOSTER, Skyline, Dinner Plate, $45.

"CLUCKERS," Rooster and Hen Salt and Pepper Shakers, $125 pair.

SUNRISE, Skyline, Sugar with lid and Creamer, $95 set.

SUNRISE, Woodcrest, Cup and Saucer, $55.

EVENTIDE, Woodcrest, Tab Bowl, $35.

EVENTIDE, Woodcrest, Dinner Plate, $55.

WEATHERVANE, Skyline, One-Tier Tidbit, $75.

"HOLLY ACRES," Woodcrest, Dinner Plate, $

WEATHERVANE, Skyline, Teapot with lid, $125. Usually has green lid.

WEATHERVANE, Skyline, 8" Square Plate, $40.

HOMEPLACE, Skyline, 8" Square
Plates, $75 each. Note difference in
hand painting.

WINDMILL, Skyline, Cup and Saucer,
$50.

RED BARN, Skyline, Cup and Saucer,
$40.

SQUARE DANCERS, Piecrust, Square
Plate, $70.

SQUARE DANCERS, Piecrust, Salad Set, which included
13" salad bowl with fork and spoon servers, 8 snack plates
with cups, each with a different dancing couple.

Stamp used as a guide for FARMER
TAKES A WIFE. Painters used the
outline as a guide for a lovely Colonial
pattern. The final result is a charming
couple framed with soft yellow sunflow-
ers painted around the edge.

FARMYARD, Woodcrest, Dinner Plate, $75. Also found on Skyline.

Tablecloth coordinating with CACTUS pattern.

CACTUS, Woodcrest, Dinner Plate, $75.

PROVINCIAL

NORMANDY, Skyline, 8" Square Plate, $45.

NORMANDY, Skyline, Sugar Bowl with lid, $40.

NORMANDY, Skyline, Platter, $75. Only piece with man and woman. The woman has been called Beatrice.

NORMANDY, Skyline, Cup and Saucer, $40.

BRITTANY, Clinchfield, Salad Plate, $45. Demi Cup and Saucer, $50.

(Top) FLOWER PICKER, 6" Square Plate, $65. (Left to right) WATERING THE FLOWERS, 6" Square Plate, $75. MILKMAID, 6" Square Plate, $75. Notice that bonnets and watering can were not painted. These plates are unique in that they were glazed prior to completion of the painting.

BRITTANY, Clinchfield, Jumbo Cup and Saucer, $75.

This Provincial set made for PV also included MAN WITH PITCHFORK and HARVESTER LADY.

SOWING SEED, 5" Square Plates, $55 each. Red or blue border.

BRITTANY, Demi Creamer, $75. (Left to right) PLOWMAN, 6" Square Plate, $60. MOWING HAY, 6" Square Plate, $60.

MISTRESS MARY, Astor, Salad Plate, $75.

MISTRESS MARY, Astor, Demi Cup and Saucer, $110. Also found with blue border on Colonial shape.

English creamer. Possible prototype for MISTRESS MARY.

MISTRESS MARY type linen towel.

LYONNAISE, Clinchfield, Demi Cup and Saucer, $85. Found with man or woman.

CALAIS, Astor, Salad Plate, $75. Similar pattern with pink borders called PICARDY.

LYONNAISE, Clinchfield, Egg Cup, $95.

LYONNAISE, Clinchfield, Dinner Plate, $80.

FRENCH PEASANT, Candy Box, $300.

FRENCH PEASANT, China Salt and
Pepper Shakers, $175 pair.

FRENCH PEASANT, Chocolate Pot,
$400.

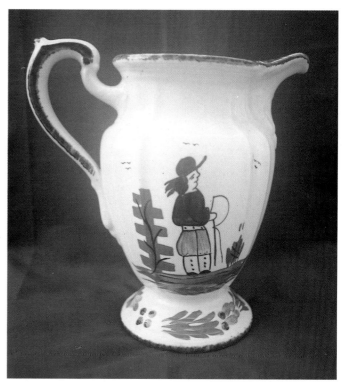

FRENCH PEASANT, Milady Pitcher,
$300.

FRENCH PEASANT, Pedestal Creamer,
$125. Sugar with lid, $75.

FRENCH PEASANT, Square Box, $150. Ash Tray, $50.

FRENCH PEASANT, Leaf Celery, $100.

FRENCH PEASANT, Dinner Plate, $125.

FRENCH PEASANT, Deep Shell, $150.

FRENCH PEASANT, 15" Platter, $250.

The FRENCH PEASANT piece, chosen sentimentally for our book cover, was the genesis for our Blue Ridge collection. Included in our collection of over 4,000 pieces are many FRENCH PEASANT pieces. The casual observer may not note the two different leaf colors painters used for the leaves in this pattern. We attribute the color difference to Southern's custom of providing retailers with their preference. It appears evident that the persimmon color leaf is found more often in the eastern United States, while the rose color, which we recognize as the color of the rhododendrons of the mountains of East Tennessee, are more often found in the southern United States.

FRENCH PEASANT, 11" Salad Bowl, $130.

Rhododendron outside the Heritage Museum in Erwin.

Chapter 7
Seasonal Patterns

Thanksgiving Blessings

PILGRIMS, Skyline, Cup and Saucer,
$40.

DRY LEAF, Leaf Celery, $45. Marked
Leaf Celery #3.

DRY LEAF, Maple Leaf Relish, $55.

THANKSGIVING TURKEY, Skyline,
Dinner Plate, $85.

THANKSGIVING TURKEY,
Clinchfield, 19" Platter, $300.

INDIAN SUMMER, Astor, Sugar with
lid and Creamer, $45 set.

TURKEY WITH ACORNS, Skyline,
Dinner Plate, $95.

TURKEY WITH ACORNS, Clinchfield,
19" Platter, $375.

TURKEY WITH ACORNS, Skyline,
Cup and Saucer, $95.

FALL COLORS, Four-section Relish
Tray, $55.

FALLING LEAVES, Colonial, Dinner
Plate, $25.

SCATTERED LEAVES, Astor, Bread
and Butter Plate, $10.

CHRISTMAS DOORWAY, Skyline, Dinner Plate, $110. Cup has the wreath, and saucer has the tree.

HOLLYBERRY, Colonial, Dinner Plate, $75.

CHRISTMAS ORNAMENT, Candlewick, Saucer, $20.

TREE WITH MISTLETOE (Left to right) Colonial, Saucer, $30. Dinner Plate, $100. CHRISTMAS TREE, Colonial, Cup, $45.

HOLLYBERRY, Colonial, Cup and Saucer, $45.

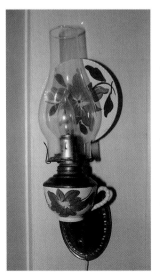

DAHLIA, Wall Lamp, $35.

DAHLIA, Candlewick, Oval Vegetable Bowl, $50.

CHRISTMAS TREE, Colonial, Dinner Plate, $100. Pattern has been found with backstamps from two different periods. Possible color variations on bows.

PETAL POINT, Skyline, Bottom of Covered Vegetable, $45.

RED FLOWER, Colonial, Bowl in aluminum basket, $40.

WINTERTIME, Skyline, Dinner Plate, $65. Snack plates with cups also produced.

"DUSTY POINSETTIA," Colonial, Dinner Plate, $60.

JINGLE BELL POINSETTIA, Piecrust, Dinner Plate, $70.

CHRISTMAS CACTUS, 13" Platter, $125. Also called GOOD LUCK.

POINTSETTIA, Demi Cup and Saucer, $30. Demi Tray, $50. Demi Teapot, $175.

Chapter 8
Cookware

Variations of ANTIQUE LEAF and LEAF in an assortment of color combinations are found on an amazing amount of cookware, that has certainly stood the test of time. Although many pieces show signs of extensive use, they are excellent shelf pieces to add to one's collection.

Appropriate backstamp used by Southern: "GLAZE FOR GLAMOROUS BEAUTY THAT CAN NEVER WEAR, FADE NOR WASH AWAY."

KITCHENETTE, Leftover Container with lid, $45. Larger leftover was also made.

Backstamp of KITCHENETTE Leftover Container.

JULIE, 8 1/2" by 12 1/2" Rectangular Baking Dish with stand, $40. JULIE was also the pattern for a round pie baker. ROCK ROSE was also a favorite cookware pattern.

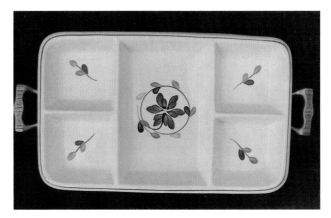

CROSS STITCH, Divided Baking Dish with stand, $40.

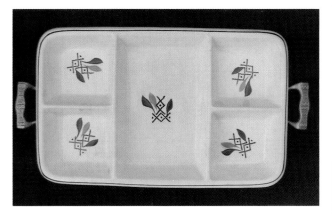

HAPPY HOME, Divided Baking Dish with stand, $40.

FULL HOUSE, Candlewick, 9" x 13" Baking Dish with stand, $50. Few Candlewick cookware pieces have been found.

Royal backstamp for FULL HOUSE baking dish.

Ovenproof backstamp used for many cookware pieces. However, not all pieces are marked.

LEAF, Waffle Set. Syrup Pitcher with lid, $75. Serving Tray, $40. Batter Pitcher, $50.

LEAF & BAR, Covered Casserole in aluminum stand, $50.

LEAF, Round, Divided Warming Dish, $45.

"RINGED LEAF," Round Baking Dish, $25.

"RINGED LEAF," Lid, $30. Fits glass jar.

ANTIQUE LEAF, Small Mixing Bowl, $25.

Backstamp on "RINGED LEAF" Round Baking Dish.

LEAF, Covered Casserole, $50. Usually came with aluminum or brass stand.

Backstamp on small ANTIQUE LEAF mixing bowl.

"RINGED LEAF," Range Shaker, Pair $50. Custard Cup, $25.

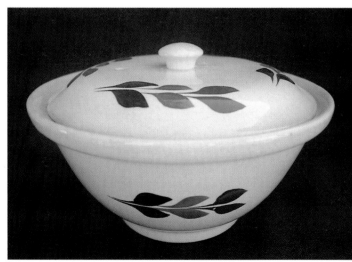

ANTIQUE LEAF, Mixing Bowl with Lid, $45. Sized to fit serving stand.

Chapter 9
China for Children
of All Ages

DEMITASSE

ROCK ROSE, Skyline, Demi Cup and Saucer, $25.

ROCK ROSE, Skyline, Demi Tray, $50.

MARDI GRAS, Candlewick, Demi Tray,
$95.

ROSEBUD, Candlewick, Demi Tray,
$95.

CAROL'S ROSES, Colonial, Demi Cup
and Saucer, $25.

MURIEL, Skyline, Demi Saucer, $10. Colonial, Demi Cup, $15. Colonial, Demi Saucer, $10.

PINK PETTICOAT, Colonial, Demi Cup and Saucer, $25.

PETUNIA, Colonial, Demi Tray, Sugar, and Creamer, $200 set.

"MOLLY," Astor, Demi Cup and Saucer, $30.

PETUNIA, Colonial, Demi Creamer, 2 1/2."

Backstamp on WEE ONE.

Backstamp on MOLLY.

WEE ONE, Astor, Demi Cup and Saucer, $30.

"JUMP UPS," Astor, Demi Cup and Saucer, $20.

192

(Left to right) DAY DREAM, Colonial, Demi Cup and Saucer, $25. BLACK-EYED SUSAN, Astor, Demi Cup and Saucer, $25.

GEORGIA, Astor, Demi Creamer and Sugar, $75 set.

PRINCESS FEATHER, Clinchfield, Demi Cup and Saucer, $30.

SKEETER, Astor, Demi Cup and Saucer, $25.

COURTSHIP, Astor, Demi Cup and Saucer, $25.

"GAIL," Clinchfield, Demi Cup and Saucer, $40.

PRETTY IN PINK, Colonial, Demi Cup and Saucer, $35.

PASTEL POPPY, Astor, Demi Cup and Saucer, $25. UCAGO backstamp.

VALLEY VIOLETS, Colonial, Demi Saucer, $10. Cup, $20. Teapot, $125.

ROXALANA, Colonial, Demi Cup and Saucer, $25.

DOGTOOTH VIOLET, Colonial, Demi Sugar, $40. ELIZA-BETH, Colonial, Creamer, $40.

RHAPSODY, Colonial, Demi Cup and Saucer, $25.

IDA ROSE, Lace Edge, Demi Cup and Saucer, $45.

"VIOLET" backstamp: "Blue Ridge Mountains Hand Art."

"VIOLET," Colonial, Demi Cup and Saucer, $45.

JONQUIL, Astor, Demi Sugar and Creamer, $70 set.

JONQUIL, Astor, Demi Teapot, $125 with lid.

"BETH ANNE," Lace Edge, Demi Cup and Saucer, $45.

"LARRY'S GARDEN," Lace Edge, Demi Cup and Saucer, $45.

Many demi cups and saucers were made for UCAGO.

SWEET CLOVER, Astor, Demi Cup and Saucer, $25.

BLUEBELL BOUQUET, Astor, Demi Cup and Saucer, $25.

YELLOW NOCTURNE, Skyline, Demi Cup and Saucer, $20.

SUNGOLD #2, Colonial, Demi Cup and Saucer, $20.

SKITTER, Colonial, Demi Cup and Saucer, $25.

RACHEL'S TULIP, Colonial, Demi Cup and Saucer, $25.

(Left to right) FOX GRAPE, Colonial, Demi Cup, $25.
CLAIRBORNE, Astor, Demi Cup, $25.

ROSEANNA, Demi Cup, $20.

SONG SUNG BLUE, Clinchfield, Demi Saucer, $20.

(Left to right) FAIRMEDE FRUITS, Clinchfield, Demi Cup and Saucer, $30. CHERRY COKE, Colonial, Demi Cup and Saucer, $25.

"TERI," Astor, Demi Saucer, $10. LE SHAY, Colonial, Demi Cup, #20.

HAWAIIAN FRUIT, Skyline, Demi Cup and Saucer, $25. FREEDOM RING, Astor, Demi Cup and Saucer, $30.

PAINTED DAISY, Colonial, Child's Tea Set, $300. Child's tea set usually consists of: 6 1/2" teapot with lid, 2" sugar, 3" creamer, 9" x 7 1/2" tray, four 6" plates, four 2" cups, and four 4" saucers.

GRANDMOTHER'S GARDEN, Colonial, Demi cup and Saucer, $25.

Demitasse collection belonging to Larry Boxum and Gail Taylor.

FRUIT SHERBET, Colonial, Demi Cup, $15.

(Left to right) MARY, Astor, Demi Cup and Saucer, $30.
FRUIT PUNCH, Colonial, Demi Cup and Saucer, $25.

BERRYVILLE, Colonial, Demi Cup and Saucer, $25.

(Left to right) CRAB APPLE, Colonial, Demi Cup and Saucer, $25. WILD STRAWBERRY, Colonial, Demi Cup and Saucer, $25.

AUTUMN APPLE, Colonial, Demi Cup and Saucer, $25. Demi Tray, $75.

WILD STRAWBERRY, Colonial, Ovide Coffeepot, $125.
Demi Creamer and Sugar $45. Demi Cup and saucer, $30.
Hand-decorated matching tablecloth.

QUARTET, Colonial, Demi Cup and Saucer, $25. APPLE
TART, Colonial, Demi Cup and Saucer, $25.

RED APPLE, Colonial, Demi Sugar, $40. QUAKER APPLE,
Candlewick, Demi Tray, $75. BIG APPLE, Skyline, Demi
Creamer, $40.

RED APPLE, Colonial, Child's Tea Set. A set consists of:
Teapot, Creamer, Sugar, Four Cups and Saucers, Four 6"
Plates, and a Tray. This beautiful set has two Trays. The
rectangular one is not often found.

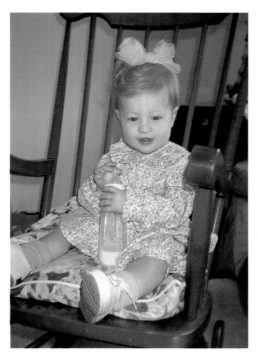

"RUFFLES," Skyline, Cereal Bowl, $75.
MISS MOUSE, Skyline, Cereal Bowl,
$75.

HUMPTY, Skyline, Cereal Bowl, $75.

Which one of these Blue Ridge dishes
shall I eat out of today?

Blue Ridge stamp for "RUFFLES."

Blue Ridge stamp of frog pattern for child's dish. None
found to date.

PIG & PALS, Divided Feeding Dish,
$125.

PIG, Astor, Plate, $95.

FRUIT CHILDREN, Cereal Bowl, $85.

FLOWER CHILDREN, Feeding Dish, $95.

PIGGY BLUES, Clinchfield, Bowl, $95.

BUNNY HOP, Feeding Dish, $125.

"HAPPY ELEPHANT," Skyline, Cereal Bowl, $75. From 3-piece Circus Set.

Astor, Child's Set: "BLUE DUCK," Bowl, $55. "BLUE LAMB," Plate, $65. PIGGY BLUES, Mug, $75.

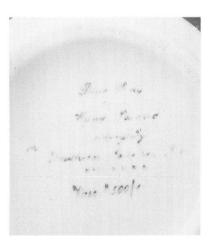

Bottom of feeding dish. 6 1/4" width and 1 1/4" deep. Stamped "500/1."

"SILLY CLOWN," Skyline, Plate, $65. Seal with ball mug completes 3-piece Circus Set, which originally sold for less than $1.

"BLUE DUCK," Astor, Cereal Bowl, $65.

"COUNTING SHEEP," Feeding Dish, $100.

Chapter 10
You Be The Judge!

Many unstamped pieces are found that have the look and sometimes, even the feel of Blue Ridge. Unlike unstamped platters and smaller pieces of dinnerware, which can linked to known pattern, they are difficult to authenticate. Sometimes, they can be verified by knowledgeable collectors or retired pottery employees. Pieces, which we were unable to positively attribute to Southern using acceptable methods of authentication, have been placed in this chapter. We have examined them and now we present them to you and extend this challenge: *Are they Blue Ridge? You be the judge!*

ART NOUVEAU, 6 1/2" Gold Trimmed, Lady Flower Frog. Gold trimmed pieces were also produced in the early years.

DOG PLANTER, 3 1/4".

ART NOUVEAU, Lady Flower Frog. Clinchfield China produced flower frogs in two sizes (6 1/2" and 8 3/4") during early production years. Some have been found with the Clinchfield Crown backstamp.

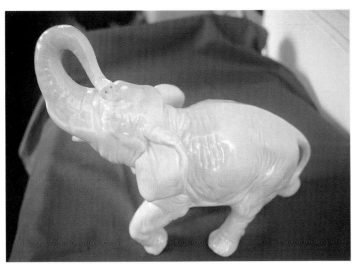

WHITE ELEPHANT, 6 1/2".

LION.

GRAY ELEPHANT, 6 1/2".

PIGS, Salt and Pepper Shakers.

PANTHER and TIGER.

SCULPTURED FRUIT, 7" Teal Pitcher. We have also seen these in other colors.

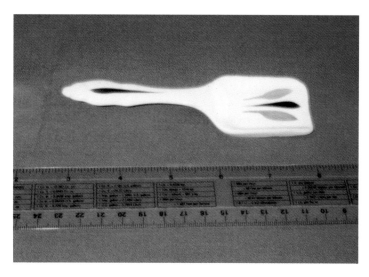

LEAF, 5 1/2" scoop. Shape is unknown but complements LEAF pattern well.

Square tile. Painting is in Blue Ridge style; tile seems to be new.

Salad Servers. Fork and spoon shapes are not recognized as Blue Ridge shapes, but the painting is in Blue Ridge style.

Egg Cup. This egg cup blends well with the two BLUE-BELL BOUQUET patterns.

Chapter 11
The Tradition Continues

Erwin, Tennessee exit sign off US 23. Hundreds of Blue Ridge collectors journey to this picturesque, friendly town to visit the site where the pottery still stands and to, what else, shop for Blue Ridge.

Hanging Elephant Antiques sign located on the side of the shop building on Main Street. "Hanging" at the elephant is always a treat. Often retired employees, who are sometimes in awe of the popularity of the wares they created so long ago, stop by with an interesting story or a rare piece of pottery.

Erwin YMCA. For many years this building has been the site of the Blue Ridge Pottery Show and Sale. The show, held each year during the Apple Festival, brings together many Blue Ridge collectors, who have never met in person, but have formed long-distance friendships through their mutual interest in Blue Ridge.

René Keplinger, co-owner of the Hanging Elephant, holding Fala, Candlewick plate, and Bird Dog, Candlewick plate. These plates were painted by Mildred Haskins Broyles. Fala was presented to Franklin D. Roosevelt by a distant cousin in August, 1940. Fala was a Scottish Terrier, who was perhaps the most publicized presidential pet up to that time.

Main Street Mall., a wonderfully rustic shop specializing in Blue Ridge.

John Hashe, owner of the Main Street Mall, is a very knowledgeable Blue Ridge collector and dealer. Wanda Hashe coordinates the Blue Ridge Pottery Club Show and Sale.

The Heritage Museum houses excellent collections of Carolina, Clinchfield, and Ohio Railroad memorabilia and rooms displaying Blue Ridge China. Tours are available from May through October.

Museum sideboard with unusual Blue Ridge teapot lamps.

Museum corner hutch with an artful display of Blue Ridge pieces.

BLUE RIDGE POTTERY CLUB
Membership Card is necessary for
early entry to show and sale.

Blue Ridge room pantry display. The Shawnee pig on the
top shelf was reportedly sent to Southern Potteries from
Ohio to serve as a pattern for a new Blue Ridge piece.
According to the museum guide the piece was never
produced.

Apple Festival 1996 handbill. This festival is held annually
during the first weekend in October.

Apple Festival Souvenir Cards made by Negatha Peterson,
who distributes them to visitors at Erwin Pottery

Negatha Peterson showing one of her own apple pitchers.

Negatha Peterson Commemorative Plate. In 1941, as a
young lady, Negatha went to work at the pottery. She
mastered the artist's techniques after only one day's
training. She was assigned to a painting crew, usually four
women, to paint stems and leaves. Today, she paints many
delightful creations of her own. In her own words, "I paint
what I like."

Hand painted Christmas cards by Negatha Peterson.

Erwin Pottery pitcher with blue duck.

1995 Christmas plate ornament.

Reverse of Christmas plate ornament with Erwin Pottery stamp. The Petersons opened Erwin Pottery after Southern Potteries closed.

Cookie Jar with Blue Ridge style pattern.

Easter Egg "Mamy" cookie jar.

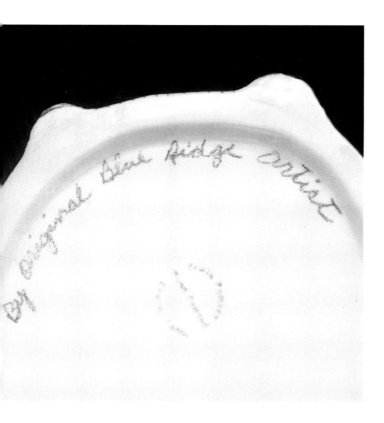

Backstamp on Erwin Pottery cookie jar. Signed "By
original Blue Ridge artist." Like several pottery artists,
Negatha perfected the skills she had learned at the pottery
and used her own enormous talent to make a living and a
name for herself. Her GOLD TOOTH "MAMY" (Negatha's
own original spelling) cookie jars have found their way into
collectors' hearts and homes and even one cookie jar
reference book.

UNCLE MOSES, cookie jar.

WASHDAY, "Mamy" cookie jar.

Personalized BLUE RIDGE collector sign, signed "Negatha P."

UNCLE MOSES, unpainted bisque.

Southern Pottery Reunion, April 26, 1996. (Photo courtesy of Charles Edwards, Erwin Record.)

SOUTHERN POTTERIES EMPLOYEES
Erwin, Tennessee, 1996

Elizabeth Rice	Ida Tiptan	Ruth Fain
Kenneth Rice	Birdie Harris	Doris Callaway
Verna Bishop	Helen Linville	Edith Tinker Hawkins
Hiram Bailey	Leona Fiskel (Roberts)	Mary Holifield
Oscar Riddle	Lena Miller	Helen & Jim Peek
Lois Johnson	Olga Bailey White	Evelyn Witcher Edwards
Mary R. Jennings	Dora Poore Lane	Violet Fain
Frankie Lewis	Blanche Poore Lane	Hazel Raznick
Sara L. Smith	Betsie Griffith Peters	Mary Hughes
Arline Sams McInturff	Charlotte Garland	John Love
Clyde Iris Keplinger	Gladys Harris	Charles Deyton
Julie M. Sparks	Mildred Miller Silvers	Agnes McInturff
Lattie Cash	Lola Johnson	Vicie Hensley Ledford
Jetta Hepson	Julia Elizabeth Johnson	Charlotte B. Tipton
Glenna Baxter Hall	Carrie Guinn	W.C. Callahan
Willie Clouse	Velma Keplinger	Ruby Hart
Pearl Ledford	Ruth S. Buchanan	Alvin "Bud" Whett
Margie Gilbert	Gertrude Shell Rice	Charles Duncan
Mayfra Barnett	Wilma Duncan	Viola Dode Garland
Margie Gray Richards	Sallie Howell	Raymond White
Charlotte Edwards	Elizabeth Reeves	

Appendix

Tout est finis!

It is finished, but it is not over. We will continue to collect. There is always time to shop for that elusive Blue Ridge piece, and always space to proudly display it. Our research will also continue. Please keep in touch and let us know what you find.

NASCO backstamp shown previously. Southern Potteries also made china for other jobbers. Backstamps for jobbers not shown in the body of this book are: VITAMIN FROLICS, SUN CHINA CO. (usually with 22 kt. gold notation), and RAJA (Union Made).

Backstamp for a pattern variation (modification). Pattern numbers (four digits) are usually found on the back of vegetable bowls.

Pattern Numbers
(To Date)

350-1	MALLARD BOX	3850	MOUNTAIN IVY	4242	GRANNY SMITH APPLE
2662	SUNGOLD #2	3852	RIDGE DAISY	4243	SCATTER PLAID
2823	SUNFLOWER	3885	AMELIA	4250	FRENCH VIOLETS
3007	FLOWERING BERRY	3887	DELICIOUS	4275	CAROLINE
3078	WRINKLED ROSE	3889	ECHOTA	4277	WEATHERVANE
3090	CHINTZ		or TWIN FLOWER	4289	BAMBOO,
3093	SEREPTA	3897	SHOO FLY		W/GREEN 4288,
3123	#7 LAZY DAZY	3898	MOUNTAIN BELLS		W/WHITE 4266
3149	CUMBERLAND	3913	DIXIE HARVEST	4321	TROPICAL W/FLOWERS
3196	DOGWOOD	3919	SOUTHERN CAMELLIA	4325	STANHOME IVY
3254	MARINER OR SAILBOAT	3920	LIGHTHEARTED	4333	NIGHT FLOWER
3272	MOUNTAIN ROSE	3925	DAHLIA	4336-	X CALICO FARM/
3274	COUNTRY ROAD	3951	POPPY DUET [3952,3953,		APPLECHECK FARM
3387	GYPSY		& 3954 similar patterns]	4340	APPLE JACK
3451	MAUDE	3954	POM POM	4340	CAROLINE
3461-4	FRUIT FANTASY	3963	JOANNA	4344	TROPICAL
3535	SUNBRIGHT	3966	CHERRY WINE	4356	KIBBLER'S ROSE
3545	POINSETTIA	4024	MOUNTAIN MEADOWS/	4358	DESERT FLOWER
3558	WILD STRAWBERRY		ALICIA	4365	SUNNY SPRAY
3583	HAT DANCER	4032	"VIVIAN"		or SERENADE
3584	SENORITA	4042	GREENBRIAR	4381	PETIT POINT
3586	CHICKEN MAN	4047	WILLOW	4382	JUNE APPLE
3588	PEANUT VENDER	4050	EVENING FLOWER	4386	EVENTIDE
3640	SWEET PEA	4051	FANTASIA		[FARMHOUSE]
3663	PEONY BOUQUET	4052	SUNNY SPRAY	4387	MING TREE
3668	POM POM	4073	RIDGE HARVEST	4390	QUILTED FRUIT
3687	"NEGATHA"	4084	SUN BOUQUET	4391	SUNRISE
3735	AUTUMN APPLE	4093	GRAY SMOKE	4419	TIC TACK
3739	PAPER ROSES	4128	BITTERSWEET	4432	WILD CHERRY #1
3743	FRUIT PUNCH	4129	VIBRANT	4479	MOUNTAIN SWEET-
3761	CAROL'S ROSES	4146	RUSTIC PLAID		BRIAR
3733	TRIPLE TREAT	4149	MAROON PLAID	4486	MOSS ROSE
	or MIRROR MIRROR	4158	PLANTATION IVY/	4489-S	LUNA
3743	FRUIT PUNCH		RIDGE IVY	4499	ROUNDELAY
3761	CAROL'S ROSES	4160	BETHANY BERRY	4512	APRIL
3770	CHERRY BOUNCE	4175	SOUTHERN DOGWOOD	4527	COUNTRY FRUIT
3773	CRAB APPLE	4195	YELLOW DOGWOOD	4532-Y	THISTLE
3775	KIBBLER'S ROSE	4225	MAYFLOWER	4553	CLAIRBORNE
3810	SUNFIRE	4226	CHEERIO	4560-Y	CLOVER
				4561-S	"TWIRLING TRIO"

Resources

Blue Ridge Beacon
7091 S. Main St.
Helen, GA 30545
(Kim & Bryan Snyder)

Blue Ridge Pottery Club
208 Harris St.
Erwin, TN 37650
(Wanda Hashe)

National Blue Ridge Collector's Directory
3737 Tyler St.
Columbia Heights, MN 55421
(Jay Parker)

National Blue Ridge Newsletter
144 Highland Dr.
Blountsville, TN 37617
(Norma Lilly)

Keillor Book and Supplement were privately published.

References

Books and Journals

The Architectural Record, "Industrial Housing Developments in America," Lawrence Veiller. Undated.

Birds, A Guide to the Most Familiar American Birds, Herbert S. Zim, Golden Press, New York, 1956.

Birds of North America, Robbins, Brunn, and Zim, Golden Press, New York, 1966.

Blue Ridge Country, "Southern Potteries, Erwin, Tennessee's Dinnerware Legacy" Diane Larkin, May/June 1994, pp. 18-19, 51.

Blue Ridge Dinnerware, Betty and Bill Newbound, Collector Books, Paducah, 1984, 1989, 1994.

Dishes What Else, Winnie Keillor, Frankfort, Michigan, 1983.

Dishes What Else, Winnie Keillor (Supplement) Frankfort, Michigan.

Collector's Encyclopedia of American Dinnerware, Jo Cunningham, Collector Books, Paducah, 1992.

Collectible Vernon Kilns, Maxine Feek Nelson, Collector Books, Paducah, 1994.

Children's Dishes, Margaret & Kenn Whitmeyer, Collector Books, Paducah, 1993.

Kovels' New Dictionary of Marks, Ralph & Terry Kovel, Crown Publishers, New York, 1986.

Periodicals - Magazines and Catalogs

American Home, 1951

Better Homes and Gardens, 1948, 1950, 1951, 1953, 1954

Country Living, 1993

Erwin Record, "Southern Potteries, Incorporated" Albert L. Price, June 30, 1976.

House Beautiful, 1942, 1947, 1948, 1949, 1950, 1951, 1952, 1953

House and Garden, 1949, 1952

Land's End Catalog, 1995

Life, November 7, 1949

Montgomery Ward Catalog, 1942, 1943, 1945, 1951, 1952, 1953, 1954, 1955

National Blue Ridge Newsletter, 1985-1996

Sears & Roebuck Catalog, 1946, 1948, 1949

Spiegel Catalog, 1948

INDEX

218

PRICE GUIDE

Prices shown are based on collectors' valuations, current shelf prices, and advertised prices for items in "mint" condition (no chips, cracks, crazing, or discoloration) at the date of publication. Prices may vary significantly based on condition, pattern, availability, popularity, and source. Most items pictured in this book have "average" prices shown in the captions for those pieces and represent neither the lowest nor highest prices for the items pictured. **PRICES SHOWN IN THIS BOOK ARE NOT INTENDED TO ESTABLISH ABSOLUTE VALUES ON ANY, OR ALL ITEMS. THE AUTHORS AND PUBLISHER DISCLAIM ANY AND ALL LIABILITY FOR ANY LOSS RESULTING FROM RELIANCE ON PRICES HEREIN.**

DESCRIPTION	FLORAL FRUIT PLAIDS LINES	COUNTRY NAUTICAL TALISMAN BIRDS	PROVINCIAL DESIGNER SEASONAL	FRENCH PEASANT
PLATES:				
14" Round	40-75			
12" Round (Cake)	30-45	60-70	90-100	100-120
10" Round (Dinner)	15-30	35-45	75-85	85-100
9" Round (Lunch)	12-15	35-45	65-75	75-85
8" Round (Salad)	10-20	30-40	60-70	70-80
7" Round (Dessert)	10-20	25-30	50-60	60-70
6" Round (B&B)	5-10	20-30	45-55	55-65
8" Round (Snack)	15-20	40-50	60-70	70-80
8" Square	25-30	45-50	85-95	95-110
7" Square	20-30	40-50	75-85	85-100
6" Square	15-30	35-45	65-75	75-85
PLATTERS:				
17"	40-75	70-100	200-350	300-350
14"-15"	25-40	110-120	175-200	225-250
12"-13"	15-25	90-100	155-180	190-200
9-10"	25-30			
Celery	10-25	45-50	50-60	70-80
Cup	5-12	15-20	30-40	40-50
Saucer	5-10	10-15	15-30	35-45
Big Cup & Saucer	30-50			
BOWLS:				
Fruit-5"	5-15	15-20	20-25	30-35
Tab -6"	15-30	25-30	30-35	40-50
Cereal-6"	5-10	15-20	20-25	30-35
Soup (7"-8")	10-20	30-35	40-50	45-55
Covered Vegetable	50-65	60-70	70-90	90-120
Vegetable (Round 8"-9")	15-30	30-40	55-65	65-80
Vegetable (Divided)	15-30	30-40	55-65	65-80
Vegetable (Oval)	15-25	30-40	50-60	60-75
Salad Bowl (10"-13")	55-75	75-85	90-100	125-140
Salad Fork	40-50			
Salad Spoon	40-50			
Gravy Boat	15-30	35-45	55-65	75-85

DESCRIPTION	FLORAL FRUIT PLAIDS LINES	COUNTRY NAUTICAL TALISMAN BIRDS	PROVINCIAL DESIGNER SEASONAL	FRENCH PEASANT
CREAMERS:				
Regular	15-25	20-40	25-50	30-75
Pedestal	50-70		80-90	90-150
SUGARS:				
Regular	15-25	25-50	30-60	45-90
Open	10-20			
Pedestal	50-70	60-80	80-90	90-100
SALT & PEPPER SHAKERS (PAIR):				
Barrel	20-25			
Skyline	25-30	45-50	40-60	
Palisades	25-30			
Woodcrest	40-50			
China	70-90			150-170
Blossom Top	70-90			
Bud Top	65-85			
Range	40-50			
Chicken		100-125		
Mallard		300-350		
Apple	30-55			
Painted Apple Shape	25-30			
Butter Dish (W/Lid)	30-35	40-85		
Butter Pat	25-30	40-45	50-55	60-65
Covered Toast	100-120	150-160	170-180	200-230
Cover Only	50-60	75-80	85-90	100-115
Plate Only	50-60	75-80	85-90	100-115
Custard Cup	10-20			
Egg Cup	20-40	30-60	40-80	
Egg Plate	25-50	75-125		
Tile/Trivet	25-40	40-60		
Cake Lifter	20-40			
Spoon Rest	30-60			
ACCESSORIES:				
Heart Relish	30-60			
Leaf Celery	40-75			100-125
Maple Leaf Relish	60-100			110-145
Loop Handle Relish	50-100			
Mod Leaf Relish	50-100			
Center Handle(4-Sect.)	50-100			
Deep Shell	50-100			120-140
Flat Shell (Bon-Bon)	50-100	130-150		
Flat Shell(Pixie/Palace)	75-125			
Martha Snack Tray	100-150			225-275
Lazy Susan (W/Holder)	400-450			
Tidbits-1 Tier	20-30	40-50	60-70	80-100
Tidbits-2 Tier	25-35	50-60	80-90	100-125
Servers(Metal/Wicker)	35-45			
Clocks	25-45			

DESCRIPTION	FLORAL FRUIT PLAIDS LINES	COUNTRY NAUTICAL TALISMAN BIRDS	PROVINCIAL DESIGNER SEASONAL	FRENCH PEASANT
TEAPOTS:				
Colonial	60-100			
Piecrust	60-80			
Skyline	50-75			
Palisades	75-100			
Woodcrest	120-150	200-225		
Ball	100-150			
Mini-Ball	150-175			
Square Round	125-140			
Chevron	120-150			
Fine Panel	125-140			
Snub Nose	100-150			
CARAFE W/STAND	45-75			
COFFEE POT (OVIDE)	85-125	150-160	250-300	300-350
CHOCOLATE POT	200-225	275-300	300-350	350-450
CHOCOLATE TRAY	500-600	750-900	900-1,000	1,000-1,200
PITCHERS:				
Martha	40-80			
Grace	75-125			165-180
Helen	80-120			
Virginia 6 1/2"	75-125			165-180
Virginia 4 1/2"	100-125			
Jane	120-130			175-190
Milady	135-160			275-300
Rebecca	120-150			
Sally	100-200			
Clara	90-100			165-180
Watauga	200-300			
Antique 5"	60-120			160-170
Antique 3 1/2"	100-125			
Alice	115-125			260-290
Abby	75-100			
Spiral 7"	75-95			
Spiral 4 1/2"	100-125			
Sculptured Fruit	90-95			
Chick (China)	115-125			
Chick (Earthen Ware)	50-55			
Betsy (China)	125-275			
Betsy (Earthen Ware)	75-125			
Betsy (Gold)	250-300			
Palisades	30-60			
VASES:				
Ruffled Top	75-100			135-150
Handled	85-115			
Bulbous (Hibiscus)	75-95			
Tapered (Mood Indigo)	95-110			150-160
Bud	135-200			
Boot	75-100			
Boot (Gold)	125-150			

DESCRIPTION	FLORAL FRUIT PLAIDS LINES	COUNTRY NAUTICAL TALISMAN BIRDS	PROVINCIAL DESIGNER SEASONAL	FRENCH PEASANT
DEMITASSE (CHILD'S):				
Teapot	125-150	150-200	200-250	225-275
Sugar	40-50	50-60	60-80	80-100
Creamer	40-50	50-60	60-80	80-100
Cup	20-35	25-35	35-50	40-55
Saucer	10-20	20-25	25-35	30-35
Tray	100-125	140-160	175-200	200-250

LAMPS:

Handled	150-200
Grecian	175-225
Teapot / Coffee Pot	100-150
Wall	75-125

BOXES (W/LIDS):

Candy (Round)	150-275
Vanity (Round)	100-200
Cigarette (Floral/Fruit)	50-100
Cigarette (Sailboat, Butterfly, Rooster)	75-110
Cigarette (French Peasant)	125-200
Seaside	175-225
Rose Step	200-250
Dancing Nude	300-400
Sherman Lily	400-500
Mallard	500-750
Ashtrays (Individual)	20-50

CHILDREN'S DINNERWARE:

Mug	30-50
Plate	75-125
Bowl	75-125
Divided Feeding Bowl	150-300
Feeding Bowl	75-150

COOKWARE:

Ramekin, Small(W/Lid)	35-45
Ramekin, Large(W/Lid)	55-70
Covered Casserole	40-60
Baking Dish (9"X13")	35-50
Batter Pitcher	75-125
Syrup Pitcher	50-100
Pie Baker (Round)	25-40
Mixing Bowl (Set Of Five)	100-175

CHARACTER JUGS:

Daniel Boone	600-750
Paul Revere	600-750
Pioneer Woman	600-750
Indian	900-1,100
Pioneer Woman (Miniature)	1,500-2,000

ARTIST SIGNED:

Platters	1,000-2,000
Plates	600-1,500

CHARM HOUSE:

Teapot	150-225
Pitcher	175-225
Ramekin (Small)	100-150
Creamer	90-100
Sugar	90-100
Salt & Pepper (Pair)	125-150

GOOD HOUSEKEEPING:

Teapot	150-165
Creamer	40-50
Sugar	40-50
Salt & Pepper (Pair)	100-130

ADVERTISING:

Dinner Plate (Decal)	30-60
B & B (Decal)	18-20
Bowl (Granny Type)	25-35
Ashtrays (Decal Only)	50-60
Ashtrays (Decal With Painted Trim)	60-75
Counter Sign (Blue Ridge)	200-250
Talisman Wallpaper (Plate)	300-500
Blue Ridge (Plate)	300-500
Primrose China (Decal-Plate)	300-500
Robert E. Lee (Decal-Plate)	200-300
Robert E. Lee (Decal-Bowl)	200-300
George Washington (Decal-Plate)	200-300

CLINCHFIELD:

Platter	10-50
Plate(Dinner)	10-50
Plate (B & B)	5-10
Cup & Saucer	10-25
Sugar	10-25
Creamer	10-25
Granny Bowl	15-45
Pitcher (Buttermilk)	40-75
Salt & Pepper (Pair)	25-45